THE EIGHT GATES OF ZEN

THE EIGHT GATES OF ZEN

SPIRITUAL TRAINING IN AN AMERICAN ZEN MONASTERY

JOHN DAIDO LOORI

EDITED BY
BONNIE MYOTAI TREACE
AND
KONRAD RYUSHIN MARCHAJ

DHARMA COMMUNICATIONS
1992

Dharma Communications
Zen Mountain Monastery
P.O. Box 156, South Plank Road
Mt. Tremper, New York 12457

9   8   7   6   5

First Edition, Fourth Printing
Printed in the United States of America

Library of Congress Catalog Card Number: 92-82977

ISBN 1-882795-00-8

The Mountains and Rivers Sutra, adapted for liturgical chanting, is reprinted with permission of Overlook Press.

The brush paintings of the ox-herding series are by Gyokusei Jikihara.

The photograph on page 2 is reprinted with permission of Adirondack Museum. Cover photograph and the photographs on pages 24, 90, 107, 113, 131, 156, 167, 193, and 220 are by John Daido Loori; on pages 11, 78, 158, 168, 209, and 210 by Sean Homon McEntee; on pages 37, 146, and 175 by Michael Joen Grey; on pages 92, 132, and 178 by Amy Shoko Brown; on page 80 by Steve Horvath; on page 194 by Walter Taiko Edge. Photographs on pages 12, 26, 38, 108, 114, 148, 272, and the back cover are from the archive collection of Zen Mountain Monastery.

Dedicated with deep gratitude to all of the teachers
who have transmitted this incredible Buddhadharma
from East to West

Nine Bows

CONTENTS

FOREWORD

I come here realizing the question of Life and Death
*   is a vital matter*
I wish to enter the Zen training program
*   of Zen Mountain Monastery*
I understand the rules of this temple
*   and assume full responsibility for maintaining them*
Please, guide me in my practice.

Since the Fall of 1980 over six hundred people have
stood at the threshold of the zendo at Zen Mountain
Monastery and read this petition aloud. The common
understanding and intent expressed at this juncture of
entry into formal training is, in one sense, the subject of
The Eight Gates of Zen. Beneath that lies a shared koan: what
exactly is being entered, who enters, how does one assume
full responsibility, how can we guide one another?

Living at the Monastery today are five of us who have
taken lifetime vows as monks, along with thirty resident
trainees. We are given a chance to take care of the teacher,
the century-old stone building, and several hundred
acres of grounds. Residents also are charged with maintaining the continuity of the daily schedule, following the
rules set out in the Doshinji Code, and running the
"business end" of the institution: the student training
program, a vigorous calendar of training retreats for
hundreds of visitors each year, a communications company, prison outreach, community service. Residents
help provide a place to train intensively and an atmosphere that is both taut with commitment, and tender

with the constant, subtle reminder that the self doesn't end with the "skin-bag."

Students living away from the Monastery, like spokes emanating from the hub of a wheel, provide the connection between the mountain and the world — reaching out with their practice into social and political relationships, and reaching back into the monastic heart, to sustain the teacher and the monks. In settings and situations that often offer little or no support for "spiritual life," the vow to be a student, to live with a student's gutsy faith, doubt and determination, takes many forms.

The koan of entry is particularized by each person who engages it. That is the critical spin on the wheel, the motion of the heart to wonder, to investigate, to offer ourselves full-out to whatever is most true. What is it that spins the wheel, that opens and enters as "gates" all that once stood as life barriers, closed places, places where our hearts would die innumerable small and large deaths? In entering this training, we are given eight directions, like illuminated pathways leading both out and in, each with a gate to be opened, each leading squarely back to the home we never leave but almost never appreciate.

Having been part of the training at the Monastery for the last ten years has been a wonderful adventure, if difficult to comment on. In the midst of it, the view is a little like the haiku by Basho:

My horse tramping
across the field, Ha!
I'm in the picture!

One thing that shouldn't be overlooked in this basically impossible project of defining, picturing, this spinning wheel of The Eight Gates, is the fact that though centered, it is undeniably in motion — an evolving process ceaselessly refining itself. One of the Monastery's most invigorating implications is the kind of energy it insists on. Nothing waits. Though the current picture may not capture all the nuances and permutations, all the history and influences, we commit to it with total conviction. Throughout the time I've been both in and observing the matrix of training here, the mysterious grace that forms around doing one's best has been the saving grace itself: technically, the Monastery should not have survived its improbable beginnings, the strains of money and personalities, the raging storm waters spilling into the dining hall during the flash flood, the bitter Catskill winters. It has been, above all, a seamless lesson in what happens when a person, human and full of all the requisite foibles, persists in practicing selflessness. Others come. Fires start in the heart. Impossible things happen, and begin to take on the clothes of ordinary beings doing ordinary things. For no rational reason, people give, take care of each other first, ask for nothing, endure hardship, offer incense to those long dead and those not yet born.

Zen teachers in this lineage have, to say the least, the oddest job around: teach what can't be taught. They're to take what is realized in the mind-to-mind transmission and express it fluidly, responding to their students' needs without necessarily sticking to any of the forms and devices used in their own training. The teaching is to take the shape of the container. On Tremper Mountain, nothing freezes for long. I watched the Zen Arts Center one day become a "spiritual community" (Zen Mountain Center) with families, dogs, cats, et. al., and then years later yet another sign being hung at the front gate: Zen Mountain Monastery, home of an increasingly demanding monasticism. The way we do what we do didn't spring forth like a full-grown animal: what is needed by the students that appear on this mountain continues to create the training, to create the teacher and his teaching.

The outward forms of the training have been a subject of much discussion over the years, with Abbot Daido

Loori often consulting with the monks or the Board of Directors, or individual students in private and public forums. The unwavering center, however, has often been maintained by the teacher alone, as he held fast to a standard of discipline that sometimes took years to appreciate for its wisdom. Recently when we set up new office space in an adjoining building to the Monastery, he watched the publications crew run full-tilt to be on time to do the meal offering and chant with the rest of the sangha. I asked why he was laughing, and he said, "I recall when I had to insist everyday that the cook even remember to do the offering. Everything was resisted. Now people run so they won't miss it. It's nice." Receiving life, offering it to life; it strikes me now as such a great gift to have a way to begin expressing that. Yet for me, like for most trainees, the process of questioning had to be gone through, repeatedly: thinking we already know, or don't need this or that part of the training, or that it is wrong or stupid. Only later does it transform, as we're sensing the intention more clearly, seeing the effect on ourselves and others, seeing the smallness and selfishness we offered when faced with a love that transmutes the tight lines of separation between "me" and "not me."

For each of the eight areas of training, our resistances test how deeply we've entered the process. Each student walks through the threshold with a bag of expectations: Zen is this, not that; liturgy is relevant for the monks, not lay people; a teacher should work this way, not that way. As our training rolls on, everything gets turned over, spilled out so we can see what we're carrying, what ideas we're dragging along the way with us. It can hurt as its happening; the poetic images often don't communicate that well. Through that passage comes a great healing, but the demands of making the journey need to be acknowledged. The nature of the self is always in question, and the eight areas of training are designed specifically to keep us wondering. If there is no self, art practice asks, how can there be self-expression? If we are free, liturgy asks, what does it matter whether the bell is struck "correctly?" If it's all one, the Precepts ask, how can there be moral action? We each tend to be surprised, though in wildly different ways. When the questions turn irrevocably personal, suddenly there is no one else who has faced these polarities and paradoxes with the same level of raw angst. Even amidst the support of sangha and teacher, there are moments, sometimes months or years, of devastating solitude.

It is at such times that the koan of "being in training" begins to work its most unnerving magic. The instruction given in dokusan after dokusan with the teacher to, "Don't tell me, show me! *Be* it," becomes the only alternative. Put the ink on the paper in art practice. Read the sutra in academic study. Don't just mouth the words during service, invoke them with the whole body and the whole mind. For those in residence, because the tendency to shut down and curl away from the pain is countered by the demands of the schedule, issues develop an incredible intensity. Sesshin happens every month. Most weekends, anywhere from thirty to fifty people arrive for retreats, and are welcomed, served, presented with the living dynamic of Zen. Because there is nowhere to hide, that which is usually hidden gets seen, acknowledged, appreciated. In this, without preaching or extolling, we guide each other with wisdom's sure hands. Whenever the purported "artifice" of the areas of training or the monastic schedule is pointed to, I find it difficult not to reflect on how much more authentic, honest, present people seem to become when they engage them. This book attempts to describe the process, how it developed, why different parts of it are important in different ways. There remains, however, an undeniable mystery to it.

Master Wu-men, author of *The Gateless Gate* koan collection, was one of the first to use the koan of entry to stir up trouble. He said,

Gateless is the Ultimate Way;
There are thousands of ways to it.
If you pass through this barrier,
You may walk freely in the universe.

That freedom is the quintessential point. We cannot deny the pain, isolation, bewilderment that color so much of human experience. We can take up the responsibility to see why we hurt, and how it may be possible to live, not only without cursing or disowning life, but with the sensitive clarity and ineffable kindness of Buddhas. Enter these gates with care — the infinite unknown expands ever ahead, and the edge of these moon-sparked blue mountains has never yet been found.

Bonnie Myotai Treace, M.R.O.
Head Monk, Zen Mountain Monastery
Mt. Tremper, New York

EDITOR'S PREFACE

John Daido Loori points out in *The Eight Gates of Zen* that Zen is essentially a matter of our lives — not an esoteric meditative technique of self-transformation, not an ancient tradition that has woven its way throughout the East, not a code of ethical conduct, not a psychology of well-being, not a certainty of any kind. There is no one to follow, no one to emulate, no one who watches, no one who cares. The practice of Zen is our response to the questions that come forth from the depths of our being. It is the struggle to access the door to the freedom of each and every moment. It is a way of using our minds amidst the outpouring of our lives. The fate of this self and of the universe rests in our hands.

Fortunately, after placing the responsibility for liberation squarely on our shoulders and underlining the futility of following any dogma, Daido Sensei then provides the collection of teachings that make up the chapters of this book. The text is a manual that encourages and instructs us on how to fix something that essentially is not broken. Its scope is large enough to address the myriad of moments. The directions are so simple that they can deal with any complexity. The components never stay the same. We provide them each time we engage this practice. The power of the book lies in its implementation.

The Eight Gates of Zen is a very modern book. It is written and read at this time in history. It always applies to us right where we are, in whatever place, situation, mood, and dilemma we may be in. It is offered one-on-

one, heart-to-heart, mind-to-mind. What it pertains to is this moment and the moment that comes around when the book is put down and we shift to any of life's activities. That is its arena of relevance. Liturgy can begin as we prepare our dinner, take the dog for a walk, get up from the subway seat at our destination. Body practice is the practice of taking a deep breath as we turn these pages. There is no theory here. It is pure life. It is our life.

The Eight Gates of Zen is a very ancient text. It reaches back to the questions that Buddha was asking himself amidst his despair and doubt, and follows the imperative that arises out of individual realization of the teachers that walked the path of this practice. Like other perennial teaching, it is simple, straightforward, and infinitely complex. It challenges the intellect and the spirit. Ingested, digested, and sweated through the pores of the body, it can transform each and every unit of life into a vivid dance of spontaneity, wisdom, and compassion.

The form of spiritual practice detailed in this book was developed and is currently implemented within the training matrix at Zen Mountain Monastery. The components, the eight areas of concentration, overlap and are dynamic in nature. They are multi-dimensional maps of activity that can be entered directly and carried everywhere. It is a very generous offering, an interrelated collection of skillful means to see oneself clearly. The description of the process could easily be ended after the chapter on zazen, the cornerstone of the practice. But, the instructions continue beyond zazen, to open up a fountainhead of areas and means of studying the self.

For a home practitioner, *The Eight Gates of Zen* is a playground that we suddenly find ourselves within. We do not have to take one step. We do not have to face in any special direction. We simply have to notice that practice can happen right where we stand; that, like it or not, it is happening right where we stand. Each instant is a real place of contact with our true nature, a place where there is harmony and out of which appropriate action can arise. The eight gates are in the kitchen when we smell the aroma of the morning cup of coffee, on the street when we greet our neighbor or curse at the driver who cut us off at the light. They are taking out the garbage and making love.

There is a revolutionary feel to this focus on the mundane as the transcendent. To appreciate clearly the radical spirit of this form of practice it is worthwhile to highlight the context within which it arises. It runs counter to the prevailing cultural norms of mindless diversions and the economic dictum of acquisitiveness and consumerism, counter to religious beliefs of dependence on and deliverance by an omnipotent deity, as well as most psychological frameworks of self definition. Instead of gimmicks, there is our immediate presence; instead of quick-fix mentality, there is thoroughness of commitment; instead of external buffers, there is uncompromising honesty.

For Buddhist practitioners, the end of this millennium has turned out to be a time that provides a reinforcing resonance for this practice. Rarely during human history have we so globally and pervasively come in contact with the realities of impermanence, interdependence, and *anatman*, the notion of no self. They are evidenced in the texture of our lives.

Our values and behaviors are a flickering kaleidoscope that is accelerating in its spin. Most of our gods are dead. Science and its extroverted child, technology, are failing to fulfill their promise of providing the panacea for suffering. Through their deepest level of inquiry and most misguided implementations they elucidate the uncertainty underlining the very existence of matter, energy, time, and space, and the certainty of perpetual flux.

As an interrelated community of beings, we are getting closer and more tightly connected as our living space becomes more crowded and communication instantaneous and broadly available. It is impossible not to notice the subtle and far-reaching interplay of cause and effect. There are no more neutral or simple solutions.

Amidst the complexities and the dissolution, the sense of the individual and collective self is crumbling. There are many questions and discomforts about who we are as individuals, families, nations, species, inhabitants of the planet, conscious beings in the vastness of the cosmos.

We have looked away from ourselves for so long that we have forgotten who we are. As we get more proficient in the game of distracting ourselves from ourselves, we continue to create a structure of the self that is alienated and always starving. We do not trust ourselves and are inheriting and perpetuating a life of anxiety, self-hatred and fear.

It is getting harder and harder to ignore the pain. The howling comes from one's heart, from the television, from the school, from the house next door. To feel the chaos and the pervasive suffering can be the turning point. We can try to run. Or we can start to practice our life and make peace with all of our demons.

This book is a collection of guidelines to let one's life be nothing other than itself, to find the deep sense of trust that is always there, to have clear understanding, and to let one's actions flow appropriately with the circumstances.

We are presented with a challenge. We are provided with well-honed tools. The technique is very simple and, in that simplicity, very difficult. The opportunity to practice it is everywhere. If it feels critical, it is. If it feels like a curiosity, it is. There is no magic in the Eight Gates; they are just a matter of how we use our mind. It is certain though, that if we engage this practice completely, we are living our lives as fully as possible, and that is miraculous.

Konrad Ryushin Marchaj

ACKNOWLEDGMENTS

This book is the result of a Zen training program that has evolved over the past fourteen years. Consequently, there is a debt of gratitude to many people, from the actual practitioners who were and are part of the unfoldment of this training matrix, to the Bodhisattvas of word processing — the editors, transcribers, and proofreaders. Principle among them are Bonnie Myotai Treace and Konrad Ryushin Marchaj, whose editorial skills accomplished the difficult task of taking the spoken word and manifesting it in book form. I also want to acknowledge my gratitude to Janice Senju Baker, Ann Hoshin Ritter, Elizabeth Jun'en Hill, and Kathy Fusho Nolan for their able words skills that helped bring this work to fruition. My thanks to Francis Cook, Philip Whalen, Ron and Cindy Green, and Nancy Edge for reading and commenting on the manuscript. A deep bow to Barry Weiss, who through the years has been a tireless resource to this sangha, and who brought this book into its camera ready form with superlative state of the art skills.

I wish to acknowledge the works of the countless scholars who are continually producing excellent English translations of basic Buddhist texts, without which much of the work involved in creating an American Zen monastic form would be virtually impossible.

Finally, my inexpressible gratitude to my teacher, Hakuyu Taizan Maezumi Roshi, for his teachings, without which this work would never have begun.

MOUNTAINS AND RIVERS ORDER

THE TEACHINGS OF MOUNTAINS AND RIVERS

Several years ago while I was practicing at the Zen Center of Los Angeles, my teacher and I worked on a book entitled *The Way of Everyday Life*. It consisted of commentaries on one of Master Dogen's major essays. We wanted to create a book that resonated with and fit the content and the spirit of the commentaries, so we put a lot of attention into the design, illustrating it with photographs that came out of my line-by-line study of the text. The result was a book that was nicely received, and we started talking about publishing a second volume, this time using as the central theme Dogen's *The Mountains and Rivers Sutra*. This sutra is a clear and profound expression of the interpenetration and mutual non-hindrance of all dualities.

The Mountains and Rivers Sutra was at the time a very obscure text; the only translation then available was a doctoral thesis done by Carl Bielefeldt, who had been a student of Suzuki Roshi in San Francisco. I got a copy of it from the library of a local graduate school and started to read and digest it. After working on it for just a very short period of time, my Dharma brother left for New York City and my teacher asked me to go along with him and help him set up a Zen Center there. The work on the book had to be put on the back burner.

A little later I moved to Mt. Tremper and established another center, starting up a sangha using the arts as a skillful means for teaching and understanding the Dharma. It happened that the building we purchased was located in a spot where there is a mountain in the back and two rivers meeting in front. According to Chinese legends such a landscape configuration denotes a place of great power and is particularly suited as a place for a monastery.

The auspicious nature of the setting recalled for me the *Mountains and Rivers* work that I had been doing with my teacher. The project took on a whole new perspective when, after being here for about a week, one morning I was in town relaxing with a copy of the *Woodstock Times* and all of a sudden I saw, printed in bold type across the top of the second page, the headline: "These mountains and rivers of the present are the manifestation of the Way of ancient Buddhas." Following that was a full page or page-and-a-half story about Dogen Zenji's *The Mountains and Rivers Sutra*. Needless to say, I was stunned, since this was a very esoteric and unknown text. How it got into the *Woodstock Times*, I had no idea. I got so excited that I didn't even read any further. I just inquired where the newspaper office was and went there immediately. Asking about the author of the article, I found out that it was the editor himself. I asked to see him and burst into his office. He said, "Can I help you?" And I blurted out, "How did you find out about Dogen Zenji?" He looked me straight in the eye and said, "Doesn't everybody know about Dogen Zenji?" As it turned out, a book entitled *Mountain Spirit* had been published by a local press, and in it was the Bielefeldt translation.

Following that incident, I began to study *The Mountains and Rivers Sutra* with renewed enthusiasm, coming back to it regularly as I encountered problems and questions that surfaced during the early years of teaching. It became a koan for me as we were organizing this place and as its shape changed from an Arts Center into a monastery.

Dogen, in bringing Zen from China to Japan, faced many of the same problems and questions that we were facing in establishing a genuine, American monastic order and training program. He was very successful in making Zen Japanese. He didn't import Chinese Zen, but rather created it for his students in a form that was essentially indigenous and contemporary. Dogen and his struggles became a model and an inspiration for me, and as I continued to dig into the sutra more and more, it became obvious that what was emerging out of it was a training matrix that covered all aspects of daily living.

In Dogen's work, when he speaks of mountains and rivers, he is not speaking just of the mountains and rivers of nature. In a way, it is about nature, the immediate landscape that surrounds us, but the mountains and rivers are not strictly the mountains and rivers of a naturalist or a field biologist. They are not the mountains and rivers of poetry and metaphor. They are not even the mountains and rivers of samsara, the ups and downs of life — but the mountains and rivers of the true Dharma, the true Dharma eye. In a sense, when you really go deeply into it you begin to realize that *The Mountains and Rivers Sutra* is not a sutra about mountains and rivers, but rather that the mountains and rivers are themselves the sutra. This is the way Dogen appreciates the mountains and rivers.

In his subtle and profound way, Dogen talks about encounters between a master and a disciple, expressing the depth and range that can exist in the teacher-student relationship. He speaks on liturgy, on body and mind unity, on how "practice and enlightenment are one." He has an extraordinary way of bringing the teachings forward, using images such as "the birth of the mountain child," "the stone woman giving birth," and "Zen fishing." Dogen's liturgy wasn't the liturgy that was common throughout thirteenth century Japan, with brocade robes and elaborate ceremonies. He emphasized the liturgy of everyday life — of washing the face, using the lavatory, cooking a meal, brushing the teeth. These activities became his liturgy, his body practice.

His appreciation of the importance of academic study as being vital to complete training also became a relevant teaching for us here at Zen Mountain Monastery. Since most of us enter Zen training knowing nothing about Buddhism, we must attend to that shortcoming and pursue the heart of the Way in academic study along with meditation. Little by little, Dogen's zazen, morality, liturgy, began to leap off the pages of *The Mountains and Rivers Sutra*, and inspire our practice, which ultimately evolved into the ten stages and the eight areas of training that are presented in this book.

This method of training and studying deals directly and experientially with the array of dualities and conflicts that have appeared in American Zen. I refer to the distinctions between monk and lay practice, social engagement and introspective isolation, men and women practicing together. The remarkable teaching of *The Mountains and Rivers Sutra* is the totally encompassing interpenetration of all dualities. These dualities have begun to be addressed in our training and form the basis of the Mountains and Rivers Order.

One of the problems that we face with Zen in America is that it has no continuity of tradition or standards. The Zen that arrived in this country has come from several places and cultures: from China, Vietnam, Japan, Korea. It has been taught by scores of teachers, and out of this evolved a real mixture of what is called Zen training. Today the training is very different as you go from center to center. There are no agreed upon guidelines of practice, no standards of transmission. There are a number of authentic lineages and a large group of unsanctioned teachers. The distinction between monks and lay practitioners has almost completely dissolved, to the point that at most centers the idea of a Zen monk has become just that — only an idea. Lay practitioners are practicing and living precisely the same as the monks. Why call one group "monks" and the other group "lay students" when there is virtually no difference between them?

What does it mean when someone has been practicing for ten years? It depends upon where he or she has practiced. Where the training center is, who the teacher is, makes a big difference in what the training is. One person who has been a monk for ten years will have done a full week's sesshin each month during that period of time. That's 120 sesshins. They will have done two 90-day intensive training periods each year. That's twenty intensive training periods during the ten-year period. They will have done hundreds of koans, lived in full-time residency, and had contact with the teacher each day, working side-by-side with him or her. This can be contrasted to another monk at another center who, during the same period of time, will have maintained a household and a full-time job, visited the teacher perhaps once a week, and done a couple of sesshins each year. When you look at these two people and say that they both have ten years of training as a monk, on the surface it appears the same, yet there is a tremendous difference between the two.

In most instances, the thrust of what Zen in America was and continues to be is zazen and the teacher-student relationship, which is the basis of the mind-to-mind transmission, common to both the Rinzai and Soto Schools. Not a lot of attention is given to other aspects of practice, particularly to the area of moral and ethical teachings, the Precepts. People "take the Precepts," but how much real training goes on in *living* the Precepts? Are the Precepts actually read, understood, engaged, lived? Are they a spiritual status symbol or the very substance of this life? There seems to be a real danger of stylizing and diluting this ageless practice to fit our fleeting fancies, to remain relatively comfortable and miss the opportunity to realize our true nature.

Throughout the history of the development of the Buddhadharma in Asia, there emerged various schools or styles of teaching that emphasized different aspects of the Dharma that was received from India. Although essentially every school and style included some sort of meditation as a basis, special emphasis was sometimes placed on other specific aspects of the training. For example, the Vinaya school emphasized the Precepts. It argued that in practicing and maintaining the Precepts and leading a moral and ethical life, one would attain enlightenment. Other schools emphasized the study of the sutras and a more academic approach to Buddhism. There were schools that emphasized the liturgy and devotional aspects of the religion, such as recitation of the Buddha's name. Some schools, such as the Obaku School of Zen, included the arts, particularly brush painting, as a way of training the monks. At Shao-lin Monastery in China, around the time of Bodhidharma, monks trained with kung-fu masters, as well as with Zen masters.

Western practitioners come to Zen with virtually no background in Buddhism. Their Japanese counterparts entering a monastery, in most cases, would have the equivalent of a Master's degree in Buddhist studies prior to beginning their monastic training. In setting up a training matrix for students at Zen Mountain Monastery and for the Mountains and Rivers Order, it was felt necessary to employ a broader spectrum of skillful means than just the traditional meditation and teacher-student relationship. As a result, what we call the "Eight Gates" of training evolved, and each of these areas of training are pursued over ten stages of spiritual development, from the very beginning with a novice student, to the final stages where formal training is completed.

With zazen at the core as the first gate, a strong teacher-student relationship is developed in the face-to-face teachings as the second gate. The third gate, academic study, explores, in addition to the sutras particularly related to Zen training, other schools of Buddhism, Buddhist history, philosophy, and psychology. The fourth gate of liturgy not only involves rites and rituals themselves, but also includes study of these practices as a direct pointing to the human mind. The fifth gate, the Precepts, is concerned not only with the ceremony of receiving the Precepts, but the continuum of ethical practice and training throughout the entire ten stages of spiritual development. In the sixth gate, art practice, not only are the traditional arts of Zen explored but also modern emerging Western Zen arts. The seventh gate, body practice, includes not only physical development of the body through exercise and martial arts, but also the teachings of Master Dogen on body and mind unity. Because the preponderance of practitioners in American Zen are lay practitioners, work practice, the eighth gate, has come to play an especially important role in training. Work is yet another way to take that which is realized and actualize it in every aspect of daily life.

Students of the Mountains and Rivers Order are expected to train and demonstrate proficiency in each of these eight areas throughout the progressive ten stages of development in order to complete formal training in the Mountains and Rivers Order. Carefully annotated training records are maintained for each student so that the question of developing proficiency is not an arbitrary one but rather a carefully tested and documented process.

This volume is an attempt to make clear the kind of training that is taking place at this particular monastery and its affiliate groups, to define the scope and depth of the training matrix and training standards of the Mountains and Rivers Order. We want to clarify the different paths of training for monks and lay practitioners, and underline the vital importance of the Buddhist Precepts within one's practice. The Mountains and Rivers Order is a spiritual organization that is designed to maintain and monitor the integrity of Zen practice for the future generations of its sangha, making it available to all those who are interested in attaining self-realization.

There are many different ways to manifest the Dharma. There are distinct religious groups that practice varied degrees of social involvement or contemplative withdrawal. Within the Christian tradition there are the Trappist cenobites living in strict isolation, the Franciscans concentrating on charity work, the Jesuits stressing the importance of education. Among Buddhists, there have been hermits living in meditative focus for years in Himalayan caves, as well as political and social activists. In establishing the Mountains and Rivers Order, we kept an open dialogue with the Christian monastics, studying the varied forms and appreciating their long history and relationship with western culture. Through the mind-to-mind transmission of the lineage holders, the Mountains and Rivers Order represents a unique interweaving of the Soto and Rinzai Zen traditions as they come to be expressed in a modern way. The training framework that is offered encourages and supports a very thorough and serious lay practice amidst present day conflicts and confusions. It also responds to the imperative and creates the possibility of a totally committed American Buddhist monastic practice.

The Eight Gates of training as presented here are an expression of the spirit of the teachings of each of the eight gates rather than the technical details of the training matrix. The Eight Gates and the Ten Stages are the ceaseless practice of Dogen Zenji's *Mountains and Rivers* — practice that engages the whole body and mind, that encompasses and fills all space and time. At Zen Mountain Monastery, this is not an abstraction but the essential condition of our lives. As it is happening here, it is intensely relevant to our basic sanity and experience of wholeness, providing clear paths for self-discovery for those who are willing to engage it.

SHAKYAMUNI'S FLOWER

Zen traces its history back to the historical Buddha, Shakyamuni. Shakyamuni's life, practice, and teachings provide the basis for most schools of Buddhism. Shakyamuni, born into a royal family in northern India, led a sheltered and comfortable life until he came in direct contact with old age, illness, and death. He became troubled, filled with doubt about the questions of life and death, questions regarding the transitory nature of all things. He did what people in India did 2,500 years ago when they were confronted with such problems — he shaved his head, put on the robe of a monk, and joined the other monks in the forest, living by begging, meditating, and looking into these questions.

At first, Shakyamuni's practice was quite ascetic. He did long periods of meditation, fasting, and doing without sleep. He practiced this way for six years, finally reaching a point of collapse due to exhaustion and hunger. When he recovered, he rejected the approach of self-mortification and denial and decided to strengthen his body. He began to accept food and he rested. His companions, the other monks, ran away from him in horror because he was rebelling against traditional methods of practice. After he nourished himself and his health returned, he began to sit in intensive meditation under the bodhi tree. And it is said that one morning, upon seeing the morning star, he realized the great enlightenment that we call *anuttara-samyaksambodhi.*

The very first words out of his mouth upon that realization were, "Isn't it incredible! All sentient beings have the

Buddha nature. At the very same moment, I and all sentient beings together enter the Way." What Shakyamuni was saying is that all sentient beings are perfect and complete, lacking nothing; that what he was looking for, what we all search for, is really right here all the time. It just needs to be realized. Immediately after that realization, he was hesitant to teach, seeing the difficulty of trying to give people something that they already have. He didn't quite know how to go about it and, at first, put off the possibility. Several of his fellow monks saw that Shakyamuni's life had been transformed, and returned to him, asking that he teach them the Way he had realized. In response to this direct request and encouragement, he began the impossible task of teaching what essentially cannot be taught.

His first teaching, the first "turning of the Dharma Wheel," had to do with the *Four Noble Truths* or the *Four Wisdoms*. The first of those *Four Wisdoms* is the wisdom of suffering. The Buddha said that life is suffering. In that statement he included all kinds of suffering: suffering due to old age and death, physical suffering, mental suffering, emotional suffering. He also included in it, to the surprise of many, suffering that comes from higher states of meditation, states of bliss, deep states of *samadhi.*

In short, what he was calling suffering were all things that are transitory. One of the basic teachings of Buddhism is that nothing is constant, everything is in a perpetual state of flux. Because things are in a constant state of change, trying to cling to them or hold on to them creates suffering. The moment we grab onto something, at that very moment we change and it changes. We try, unsuccessfully, to hold onto all sorts of things: material things, mental things, spiritual things.

The Second Noble Truth, the Second Wisdom that the Buddha taught, is that the cause of suffering is thirst.

"Thirst" is used here to indicate desire, clinging, holding on, craving. That attachment comes from the illusion that there exists a separate self, a separate entity that is distinct from all other things.

The fundamental aspect that makes Buddhism unique and distinct from all of the other religions, past and present, is that it is based on the principle of *anatman*, no self. Other religions thus far in history are based on the idea of a self, the idea that there exists an entity called the self. Buddhism says that there is no self. And if you examine this question yourself — what is the self? — you'll find that the best you can come up with is a list of aggregates. My self is my body, my mind, my memory, my history, my experience. But those are aggregates in the same way that walls, ceiling, floor, doors, windows are aggregates that describe a room. They don't address the question of what is "selfness" itself, what is "roomness" itself, what is "chairness" itself, "treeness" itself.

When you take away the aggregates, what is it that remains? In Western philosophy it is said that when you take away the aggregates, what remains is an essence; an essence of a room, a chair, a tree. Likewise, there is an essence of a self and, in the Judeo-Christian tradition, that self-essence is called the soul. Soul is a postulation; it's a premise upon which much of Western philosophy and logic are based. In Buddhism, the enlightenment experience of the Buddha and of thousands of Buddhist men and women over the past 2,500 years confirms that beyond the aggregates, nothing remains. The self is an idea. It is in a constant state of change.

Who you are now is not who you were when you were three months old. You don't look the same, think the same, feel the same, act the same. The same can be said for you now and who you will be at eighty years of age — you won't look the same, feel the same, think the same, act the same. From a physiochemical point of view, there isn't a single atom or molecule in your body right now that was there five years ago. The face of a friend that you see today is different than it was in the past. And so are you.

So, what is the self? What is it that sits here? What is it that thinks and feels? What we usually call the "self" is this bag of skin; we consider everything inside the bag of skin to be "me" and everything outside of it to be the rest of the universe. When we separate ourselves from the rest of the universe, then, obviously, everything we need is out there, outside our self. And so, the consequences of the illusion of self are desire, thirst, craving, need — which in turn form the roots of suffering.

The Third Noble Truth of the Buddha is that it is possible to put an end to suffering. There is a certain logic that exists here: if suffering exists, then it must have a cause. The Second Noble Truth identifies the cause of suffering. The logic continues: once you say a thing exists, there also always exists the possibility of its non-existence. That is the Third Noble Truth, the cessation of suffering. And if something exists and then it ceases to exist, there must be a process, a path, a way for that transition to happen. This process is the Fourth Noble Truth, the Eightfold Path of the Buddha. That Eightfold Path forms the basis of everything contained in the Buddha's forty-seven years of teaching. Though it manifested in a variety of shapes and forms, everything he taught was none other than the Way outlined in the Four Noble Truths, his very first teaching.

The Four Noble Truths, the Eightfold Path, all the things we do in Zen Buddhist training, are called *upaya*, or "skillful means," ways to get us to see that the truth we seek is already present. Ultimately, there is nothing to teach, no one to give, and no one to receive. In fact, there are no Zen teachers, because the truth is this very life itself. But reading, understanding, or believing that the truth is this very life itself is very different from *realizing* that the truth is this very life itself — very different indeed.

"The truth of the Buddhadharma cannot be reached by words and letters." When the true essence of Buddhism crossed over to China in the sixth century A.D., carried there by the Indian monk Bodhidharma, these are the words he used to point the Way. When Bodhidharma arrived in China, the institution of Buddhism had already existed there for three hundred years. Many temples had been built, rich patrons were supporting the monks, the relatively "new" religion was a rage. Most significantly, the ruler of China, Emperor Wu, was a Buddhist, which meant that Buddhism was recognized nationally. Emperor Wu was also a scholar of Buddhism. He had texts translated and studied them extensively. He knew the writings well. In all of the temples, the monks were busy reading the sutras, contemplating the teachings, studying Buddhism.

When we want to find out about something new, what do we do? We buy a book and read it. We figure if we can name it or describe it, we understand it and possess it. For the most part, in most endeavors, we can get away with that kind of approach. But that doesn't work in Zen. It is the direct experience, not the words and ideas that describe it, that Zen is all about. When Emperor Wu heard that the famous Indian monk Bodhidharma had arrived in China, he immediately sent for him. The great Emperor Wu bragged to Bodhidharma about all the wonderful deeds he had accomplished in spreading Buddhism in China — how he had built monasteries and translated sutras. Wu asked what merits he had attained by virtue of his beneficent activity; Bodhidharma responded, "No merit whatsoever." At this, Emperor Wu became defensive and wanted to test Bodhidharma to see how deep his understanding was, so he asked him, "What is the first holy principle of the enlightened teachings?" Bodhidharma said, "Vast emptiness, nothing holy." Bodhidharma was pointing to the very same truth that the Buddha pointed to — the self is empty, the ten thousand things are empty, delusion is empty, enlightenment is empty, Buddhism is empty. And it is because Buddhism is empty that it can manifest itself in ten thousand ways. It is because of emptiness that we can speak of enlightenment and delusion.

Emperor Wu said, "Then who are you, standing here before me?" Bodhidharma replied, "I don't know." With that, he turned and left, crossed the Yang-tze River and came to Shao-lin Monastery. At Shao-lin he sat for nine years facing the wall and doing zazen. When Bodhidharma said, "I don't know," he was expressing intimacy with the ten thousand things, the intimacy of forgetting the self.

We say, "To study the Buddha Way is to study the self, and to study the self, ultimately, is to forget the self." What happens when you forget the self? What is it that remains when there is no longer a self? Everything. Everything remains. The whole phenomenal universe remains. The only difference is that there is no longer a separation between you and it. That is a very radical way of perceiving your life and the universe. It affects the essence of your being, changing the way you function, relate, understand yourself and all other things. It is that experience that we call enlightenment, the real intimacy of no separation between self and other. When there is no separation, there is no knowing. You need to have two things in order to know: a knower and what the knower knows. You need a reference system, a context. In unity, there is no knowing; there is no knower and no thing that the knower knows. There is only the one reality. So Bodhidharma's, "I don't know," was another way of saying precisely what he had said in his first response: "Vast emptiness, nothing holy."

At Shao-lin, Bodhidharma put forth the four points that have defined Zen Buddhism from that time until the present, — "Zen is a special transmission outside the scriptures, no reliance on words and letters, a direct pointing to the human mind, the realization of Buddhahood." The first point — "a special transmission outside the scriptures" — is a unique and central aspect of Zen training. It does not mean that the transmission depends on an oral tradition as opposed to a written tradition. It means mind-to-mind. It means that the scriptures and discourses contain the words and the ideas that describe the reality of Shakyamuni's religious experience, his enlightenment, but that what needs to be transmitted is not the description, but the very thing itself. In other words, it means that Shakyamuni Buddha's enlightenment experience is to be the experience of each and every practitioner.

The second point is "no reliance on words and letters." In general, our way of doing things is very dependent on words. We seem to believe that to name a thing is to know it. But all of the naming in the world, all of the quoting of sutras, all the paraphrasing of past teachings, doesn't cut it when it comes to the enlightenment experience. It is only the experience itself that is actually transformative. To understand it or to believe it doesn't impart any lasting strength—but to realize it, to make it real for yourself, can transform your life.

The third point, "direct pointing to the human mind," brings us back full circle to the Eightfold Path outlined in the Buddha's first teaching on how suffering can be brought to an end. The Eightfold Path at Zen Mountain Monastery translates itself into the eight areas of training that are going on here each day, each week, each month, each year. The training is the same for monks and lay practitioners, and the heart of it — the foundation and bottom line of our training — is zazen. With time, zazen begins to function as the liturgy, in services involving chanting and bowing. It also manifests in academic study, the study of the sutras, understanding that these contain descriptions of the reality of enlightenment, not yet the reality itself. The Precepts, the moral and ethical teachings of the Buddha, are also part of that Eightfold Path, as are body practice, art practice, and work practice. Experiences in each of these areas are continuously processed through what we call Zen study, the face-to-face study with the teacher. Our training is based on these eight areas, on understanding their roots and their relevance in our lives at this time and place. And the aim of the training is "the realization of Buddhahood," personally, intimately, by each practitioner.

One of the skillful means used in the Zen tradition to encourage practitioners to realize themselves is known as koan study. After a student has developed a certain level of concentration (or *joriki*), a koan may be introduced by the teacher as a point of focus. Koans are apparently paradoxical statements or questions that cannot be realized by the intellect alone. The apparent paradox is a function of language: in reality there are no paradoxes. Paradox only appears in the words and ideas that describe reality. A typical koan might be: "You know the sound of two hands clapping; what is the sound of one hand clapping? Don't tell me about it; show me!" Or: "What is your original face, the face you had before your parents were born? Again, don't tell me; show me!"

But these questions — the sound of one hand clapping, the original face — are no different than the questions, "Who am I?" "What is life?" "What is truth?" "What is reality?" "What is God?" — the very questions that moved Shakyamuni to start his spiritual search. They all address the ground of being, the ultimate nature of reality. When working with a koan, all kinds of issues may arise, and the student will need to work with each one of them. As barriers arise, one learns to acknowledge them, to understand them intimately, to let them go. And little by little, all of the "stuff" that creates the illusion of the self begins to fall away. The everyday mind constantly reaffirms the idea of the self; when the mind stops moving, the self is forgotten.

But the condition of "self is forgotten; all things are one" does not function. In fact, someone who is stuck in the experience of the unity of all things would have a great deal of difficulty crossing the street without getting hit by a car. You have to be able to differentiate in order to survive. What you realize through practice is that the whole universe is one reality, that you and I are the same thing. But then we need to go further and take the next step; that is, I am *not* you and you are *not* me. Both of these facts, oneness and differentiation, exist simultaneously and interpenetrate perfectly.

When we start our practice, it is like climbing a mountain. We move a few feet ahead and then slide back a few feet. We repeat the process and gradually work our way to the peak, the enlightenment. The view is vast, boundless, with no hindrances. But the practice doesn't end there, at least not in Mahayana Buddhism. You have to keep going when you reach the peak. Our life is not about sitting on some mountaintop contemplating our navel. It takes place in the world, interacting with others. The question becomes how to proceed when we are on the top of the mountain. We go straight ahead, and straight ahead takes us right back down the other side, into the valley, into the market place. It is there that our realization functions and manifests itself in everything that we do; in the way we drive a car, raise a child, maintain a relationship, grow a garden, live a life. If our practice doesn't function there, what good is it? Why are we doing it?

Realizing the nature of the self, the ground of being, is *prajna* or wisdom. When we realize the nature of the self, we also realize that what we do and what happens to us are the same thing, that cause and effect are one. And when you really see what that means, what follows is a deep sense of responsibility. A sense of responsibility is born not only for yourself but for the whole phenomenal universe; not only for what's going on here, but for what's happening in Europe and in Africa, for what's happening in Alaska and South America and the Middle East; not only at this time but in the past and in the future. When we truly embrace that sense of responsibility, we at once empower ourselves. It sounds on the surface like this is a terrible burden, but actually it is liberation. For example, when I really understand that I am responsible, then I can no longer blame, I can no longer say "He made me angry!" because I know only I can make me angry. That simple realization empowers me to do something about anger. As long as someone else made me angry, I'm just a victim of circumstances I can do nothing about. Through realizing our responsibility, we empower ourselves to change our life, to bring it in accord with the Way.

Implicit in wisdom is its activity: compassion. They are inseparable. Compassion is the functioning of wisdom. We should understand that compassion is not the same as intentionally doing "good," but that it happens the same way you grow your hair: there is no effort involved, no sense of separation, no giver or receiver. It is just one reality: the action itself.

My Dharma grandfather, Yasutani Roshi, had a wonderful way of describing how compassion functions. He used the hands as an example. You take an ego and give it to each hand — give your left hand "left hand ego" and your right hand "right hand ego." Now, if you put money in the left hand, the right hand wants to know how come the left hand always gets all the money, why doesn't anybody put money in the right hand? If the left hand were to get caught in a fire — I'm throwing logs into the stove and my sleeve hooks and I can't get the hand out and it's screaming in pain — the right hand wants to help, but it may hesitate. Depending on whether the fire is too hot, it may decide to help or it may decide not to risk it. But when you enlighten these hands — when they realize that they are two parts of the same reality, me — then, when money is placed in the left hand, the right hand doesn't mind. If the left hand has it, the right hand has it. But "You have it therefore I have it" doesn't make sense unless you know that you and I are the same thing. When the left hand gets caught in the fire, the right hand doesn't hesitate a second; it immediately responds. If the left hand is burning, the right hand is burning. But this is true only if you realize they are the same thing. And when you really understand that, what you understand, profoundly and deeply, is responsibility. That sense of unity is the basis of compassion. You take care of everything like you take care of yourself. In a way it is very self-centered, except that the self now consumes the whole universe. Nothing is left out.

Every one of us is conditioned from birth, programmed by our parents, teachers, peers, education, and culture. By the time we reach adulthood, we're living out of a program, responding to circumstances like robots. We do not know who we are or what our life is. Yet, underneath all the conditioned patterns is a person. What Zen is about is peeling back the layers of conditioning and getting to the ground of being. It is about realizing that ground of being and learning to live one's life out of what we directly, personally, and intimately experience of ourself and our life, rather than out of what we've been told we should or shouldn't be.

The attainment of our true nature is something that no one can give to us; each person has to do it alone. Zen is a process for doing it, a 2,500-year-old process. It wasn't invented yesterday. It is not a fad. It has been tested by innumerable practitioners on virtually every continent on the face of the Earth and now it is here, in this country, and we have the opportunity to try it. It is simple and direct and very difficult. It challenges us to be with ourselves, to study the self, to forget the self, and to be one with the ten thousand things.

Zen is not Japanese and it's not Chinese. It is American. It didn't come from Asia; it has always been here. It is a way of using your mind and living your life and doing it with other people. Unfortunately, nobody can supply a rule book to go by, because what it is about can't be spoken of, and that which can be spoken of is not it. So, we need to go very deep into ourselves to find the foundations of it. Zen is a practice that has to do with liberation, not some kind of easy certainty. The wisdom of that liberation not only affects our lives, but the lives of all who we come in touch with, all that we know, and all that we do.

THE SEAT OF ENLIGHTENMENT

Zazen is a particular kind of meditation, unique to Zen, that functions centrally as the very heart of the practice. In fact, Zen Buddhists are generally known as the "meditation Buddhists." There are many different ways to study the Buddha Way and to realize oneself. There are groups of Buddhists who primarily use what is called the *vinaya*, or moral precepts of the religion, as the focus. There are schools that emphasize academic study. In Zen the emphasis is on zazen; it's at the core of the whole practice. We do get involved in the other aspects of Zen training, but we always return to the heart of the matter — zazen.

Basically, zazen is the study of the self. The first stage of zazen has the appearance of being what we ordinarily understand as meditation and, as a consequence, we often call it meditation. But it is important to understand that, actually, zazen is not just meditation. It's not contemplation, introspection, or the quieting and focusing of the mind. Zazen is sitting Zen. There are also walking Zen, working Zen, laughing Zen, and crying Zen. As Gary Snyder said, "Zen is a way of using your mind, living your life, and doing it with other people."

The great Master Dogen said, "To study the Buddha Way is to study the self, to study the self is to forget the self, and to forget the self is to be enlightened by the ten thousand things." To be enlightened by the ten thousand things is to recognize the unity of the self and the ten thousand things. Upon his own enlightenment, Buddha was in seated meditation; Zen practice returns to the same seated meditation again and again. For two thousand five hundred years that meditation has continued, from generation to generation; it's the most important thing that has been passed on. It spread from India to China, to Japan, to other parts of Asia, and then finally to the West. It's a very simple practice. It's very easy to describe and very easy to follow. But like all other practices, it takes doing in order for it to happen.

Most of us are preoccupied. We're constantly carrying on an internal dialogue, constantly talking to ourselves. As long as we're involved in that conversation, we tend to miss the moment-to-moment awareness of our life. We look but we don't see; we listen but we don't hear; we eat but we don't taste; we love but we don't feel. All of the data is there — the senses are receiving all of the information — but somehow cognition is not taking place. Zazen brings us back into the moment, which is exactly where our life takes place. It can be said that if we miss the moment, we miss our lives. And the central part of the moment is our breath; therefore, the breath becomes the key to zazen.

We tend to see body, breath, and mind separately, but in zazen they come together as one reality. The first thing to pay attention to is the position of the body in zazen. The body has a way of communicating outwardly to the world and inwardly to oneself. How you position your body has a lot to do with what happens with your mind and your breath. Throughout the years of the evolution of Buddhism, the most effective positioning of the body for the practice of zazen has been the pyramid structure of the seated Buddha. Sitting on the floor is recommended because it is very stable. We use a zafu — a small pillow — to raise the behind just a little, so that the knees can touch the ground. With your bottom on the pillow and two knees touching the ground, you form a tripod base that gives three hundred and sixty-degree stability.

There are several different leg positions that are possible while seated this way. The first and simplest is the Burmese position, in which the legs are crossed and both feet rest flat on the floor. The knees should also rest on the floor, though sometimes it takes a bit of exercise to be able to get the legs to drop that far. If they can't, try what is commonly known as the tailor position. Japanese tailors sit with their legs crossed but with the knees still up. After awhile the muscles will loosen up and the knees will begin to drop. To help that happen, sit on the front third of the zafu, shifting your body forward a little bit. By imagining the top of your head pushing upward to the ceiling and by stretching your body that way, get your spine straight — then just let the muscles go soft and relax. With the buttocks up on the zafu and your stomach pushing out a little, there will be a slight curve in the lower region of the back. In this position, it takes very little effort to keep the body upright.

Another position is the half lotus, where the left foot is placed up onto the right thigh and the right leg is tucked under. This position is slightly asymmetrical and sometimes the upper body needs to compensate in order to keep itself absolutely straight. By far the most stable of all the positions is the full lotus, where each foot is placed up on the opposite thigh. This is perfectly symmetrical and very solid. Stability and efficiency are the important reasons sitting cross-legged on the floor works so well. There is absolutely no esoteric significance to the different positions. What is most important in zazen is what you do with your mind, not what you do with your feet or legs.

There is also the seiza position. You can sit seiza without a pillow, kneeling, with the buttocks resting on the upturned feet which form an anatomical cushion. Or you can use a pillow to keep the weight off your ankles. A third way of sitting seiza is to use the seiza bench. It keeps all the weight off your feet and helps to keep your spine straight. Finally, it's fine to sit in a chair, though it's important to use a cushion rather than to sit on the hard surface of the chair, and to keep your feet flat on the floor. You use the cushion, or zafu, the same way you would use it on the floor — sitting on the forward third of it. It's very important to keep the spine straight with the lower part of the back curved. All of the aspects of the posture that are important when seated on the floor or in seiza are just as important when sitting in a chair.

The importance of keeping the back straight is to allow the diaphragm to move freely. The breathing you will be doing in zazen becomes very, very deep. Your abdomen will rise and fall much the same way an infant's belly rises and falls. In general, as we mature, our breathing becomes restricted, and less and less complete. We tend to take shallow breaths in the upper part of the chest. Usually, we've got our belts on very tight or we wear tight clothing around the waist. As a result, deep, complete breathing rarely occurs. In zazen it is important to loosen up anything that is tight around the waist and to wear clothing that is non-binding. For instance, material should not gather behind the knees when you cross the legs, inhibiting circulation. Allow the diaphragm to move freely so that the breathing can be deep, easy, and natural. You don't have to control it. You don't have to make it happen. It will happen by itself if you assume the right posture and position your body properly.

Once you've positioned yourself, there are a few other things you can check on. The mouth is kept closed. Unless you have some kind of a nasal blockage, breathe through your nose. The tongue is pressed lightly against the upper palate. This reduces the need to salivate and swallow. The eyes are kept lowered, with your gaze resting on the ground about two or three feet in front of you. Your eyes will be mostly covered by your eyelids, which eliminates the necessity to blink repeatedly. The chin is slightly tucked in.

Although zazen looks very disciplined, the muscles should be soft. There should be no tension in the body. It doesn't take strength to keep the body straight. The nose is centered in line with the navel, the upper torso leaning neither forward nor back. The hands are folded in the cosmic mudra. The dominant hand is held palm up holding the other hand, also palm up, so that the knuckles of both hands overlap. If you're right-handed, your right hand is holding the left hand; if you're left-handed, your left hand is holding the right hand. The thumbs are lightly touching, thus the hands form an oval, which can rest on the upturned soles of your feet if you're sitting full lotus. If you're sitting Burmese, the mudra can rest on your thighs. The cosmic mudra tends to turn your attention inward.

There are many different ways of focusing the mind. There are visual images called mandalas that are used in some traditions as a point of concentration. There are mantras, or vocal images. There are different kinds of mudras used in various Eastern religions. In zazen, we focus on the breath. The breath is life. The word "spirit" means breath. The words "ki" in Japanese and "chi" in Chinese, meaning power or energy, both derive from breath. Breath is the vital force; it's the central activity of our bodies. Mind and breath are one reality: when your mind is agitated your breath is agitated; when you're nervous you breathe quickly and shallowly; when your mind is at rest the breath is deep, easy, and effortless.

It is important to center your attention in the *hara*. The hara is a place within the body, located two inches below the navel. It's the physical and spiritual center of the body. Put your attention there; put your mind there. In the West we have a tendency to keep our attentiveness focused on our face, because that's what we project to the world. We're always aware of our face. That's why, when you do something embarrassing, the blood immediately rushes to the face and you blush. As you develop your zazen, you'll become more aware of the hara as the center of your attentiveness. You'll walk from the hara, work from the hara and, when you get embarrassed, you'll have a warm hara instead of a red face. The hara will become a center of power in the body. The same association that you make with it in zazen as the still point can be made when something unusual or unexpected happens. Rather than scattering your energy, you'll find that almost automatically it will center in the hara. You'll have found and developed the still point out of which all the activity of your life, all the actions that must be taken, naturally arise.

When you take your seated position and assume the proper posture, put your attention in the hara. Begin rocking the body back and forth, slowly, in decreasing arcs, until you settle at your center of gravity. The mind is in the hara, hands are folded in the cosmic mudra, mouth is closed, tongue pressed on the upper palate. You're breathing through the nose and you're tasting the breath. Keep your attention on the hara and the breath. Imagine the breath coming down into the hara, the viscera, and returning from there. Make it part of the whole cycle of breathing.

We begin working on ourselves by counting the breath, counting each inhalation and each exhalation, beginning with one and counting up to ten. When you get to ten, come back to one and start all over. The only agreement that you make with yourself in this process is that if your mind begins to wander — if you become aware that what you're doing is chasing thoughts — you will look at the thought, acknowledge it, and then deliberately and consciously let it go and begin the count again at one.

Let's say you're sitting, counting the breath and when you reach the number four, suddenly you hear a fire engine going by. The minute you hear the fire engine, the mind immediately starts a whole series of thoughts. "It's going up the street. The fire must be up that way. I'll bet it's that third house on the right. I knew that house was going to catch fire. It's an obvious fire trap. I hope those kids that were playing outside are not in it. Isn't it awful that those people don't take care of their property." Soon you've developed a full-blown scenario and you're thousands of miles away from the breath, totally involved in the imaginary fire. When you realize that you've drifted, first acknowledge the thought, then deliberately and consciously release it, let it go, and bring your attention back to the breath, starting the counting at one.

The counting is a feedback to help you know when your mind has drifted off. Each time you return to the breath you are empowering yourself with the ability to put your mind where you want it, when you want it there, for as long as you want it there. That simple fact is extremely important. We call this power of concentration *joriki*. Joriki manifests itself in many ways. It's the center of the martial and visual arts in Zen. In fact, it's the source of all the activity of our lives.

When you've been practicing this process for a while, your awareness will sharpen. You'll begin to notice things that were always there but escaped your attention. Because of the preoccupation with the internal dialogue, you were too full to be able to see what was happening around you. The process of zazen begins to open that up. It begins to make you aware of your body and your mind. That awareness can be a very powerful force in everything you do; in how you practice a relationship, raise a child, drive a car, do a job, live your life. It's really important not to miss the present. Zazen has to do with that process of being in the moment.

When you're able to stay with the counting and repeatedly get to ten without any effort and without thoughts interfering, it's time to begin counting every cycle of the breath. Inhalation and exhalation will count as one, the next inhalation and exhalation as two. This provides less feedback, but with time you will need less feedback.

Eventually, you'll want to just follow the breath and abandon the counting altogether. Just be with the breath. Just be the breath. Let the breath breathe itself. That's the beginning of the falling away of body and mind. It takes some time and you shouldn't rush it; you shouldn't move too fast from counting every breath to counting every other breath and on to following the breath. If you move ahead prematurely, you'll end up not developing strong joriki. And it's that power of concentration that ultimately leads to what we call *samadhi*, or single-pointedness of mind.

In the process of working with the breath, the thoughts that come up, for the most part, will be just noise, just random thoughts. Sometimes, however, when you're in a crisis or involved in something important in your life, you'll find that the thought, when you let it go, will recur. You let it go again but it comes back, you let it go and it still comes back. Sometimes that needs to happen. Don't treat that as a failure; treat it as another way of practicing. This is the time to let the thought happen, engage it, let it run its full course. But watch it, be aware of it. Allow it to do what it's got to do, let it exhaust itself. *Then* release it, let it go. Come back again to the breath. Start at one and continue the process. Don't use zazen to suppress thoughts or issues that need to come up.

Scattered mental activity and energy keeps us separated from each other, from our environment, and from ourselves. In the process of sitting, the surface activity of our minds begins to slow down. The mind is like the surface of a pond — when the wind is blowing, the surface is disturbed and there are ripples. Nothing can be seen clearly because of the ripples; the reflected image of the sun or the moon is broken up into many fragments.

Every other creature on the face of the Earth knows how to just shut up and sit: a butterfly on a leaf, a cat in front of a fireplace. Even a hummingbird comes to rest sometimes. But humans seem to be constantly on the move all day long. Even during the night we have to dope ourselves just to fall asleep. We seem to have lost the ability of our primitive ancestors to just be still with ourselves.

Out of that stillness, our whole life arises. If we don't get in touch with it at some time in our life, we will never get the opportunity to come to a point of rest. In deep zazen, deep samadhi, a person breathes at a rate of only two or three breaths a minute. Normally, at rest, a person will breathe about fifteen breaths a minute — even when we're relaxing, we don't quite relax. The more completely your mind is at rest, the more deeply your body is at rest. Respiration, heart rate, circulation, and metabolism slow down in deep zazen. The whole body comes to a point of stillness that it doesn't reach even in deep sleep. This is a very important and very natural aspect of being human. It is not something particularly unusual. All creatures of the earth have learned this and practice this. It's a very important part of being alive and staying alive: the ability to be completely awake.

As you continue the process of letting go and bringing your mind back to the breath, the breath will slowly get deeper and easier. The mind will slowly begin to quiet down and the surface of that pond will become like glass, like a mirror that reflects and doesn't process — it just reflects. When there is a flower in front of it, it reflects a flower. When the flower is gone, the reflection is gone. When it hears a fire engine go by, it hears the fire engine. When the sound of the fire engine fades, the reflection dissolves and the smooth surface returns. It's always open, receptive, aware. It doesn't hold on, attach, or cling. It's free at every moment.

Once the counting of the breath has been really learned, and concentration, true one-pointedness of mind, has developed, we usually go on to other practices such as koan study or *shikantaza* ("just sitting"). This progression should not be thought of in terms of "gain" or "promotion"; that would imply that counting the breath was just a preparation for the "real" thing. Each step is the real thing. Whatever our practice is, the important thing is to put ourselves into it completely. When counting the breath, we just count the breath.

It is also important to be patient and persistent, to not be constantly thinking of a goal, of how the sitting practice may help us. We just put ourselves into it and let go of our thoughts, opinions, positions — everything our minds hold onto. The human mind is basically free, not clinging. In zazen we learn to uncover that mind, to see who we really are.

It's no small thing to be born human. A lot of "stuff" comes along with the opportunity of human life. Zazen is an incredible doorway for getting to the bottom of it all, and learning to live your life out of what you directly experience yourself: not what somebody tells you, not what you read, not because you should, but because your own direct experience of yourself and your life tells you what to do.

TEN STAGES

In the traditional Zen monasteries of Asia, training was seemingly an organic process. Although the teacher knew what was going on, that is, where students were in terms of their understanding and what they still needed to realize, the students didn't necessarily know this. With the arrival of Japanese teachers in the West, this approach continued. I went through my entire training without any gauge of where I was, what I needed to do, or where the gaps were, other than from what came up in *dokusan* (private interviews with the teacher). And, usually, there was very little if any dialogue in dokusan, because it primarily involved working directly with a koan. The teacher would either indicate that I should go on to the next koan or urge me to go deeper with the one I was working on. There was very little sense of what was going on. This tradition of teaching a student without providing a reference point is deeply ingrained in the East. But it is not so easily embraced in the West, where we are obsessed with wanting to know how we are doing, and with having some way of measuring our progress and comparing ourselves with others.

In ancient Japan, if you wanted to study the martial arts, you would go to a master and ask to become a student. If the master accepted you, you began your training. The training would continue for any number of years until, at some point, the master would say that you were ready and could start teaching on your own. When you began training you would receive a white belt to hold your *gi* together. As you practiced for many, many years, that white belt would get very dirty, because it is the one part of the uniform that can't be washed. After six or seven years of putting the gi on and taking it off every day, your white belt would have become so stained that it could only be called a black belt. You became "the black belt" along with your uniform. It was a gradual, almost indiscernible process. The wide range of colored belts we now associate with progress in the martial arts was invented only recently, primarily for Westerners who seemed to need a well-defined sense of their place in the hierarchy. So now there are yellow belts and green belts and brown belts and blue belts, in addition to the white belt of the beginner and the black belt of the accomplished practitioner.

A similar situation was encountered in Zen. In my days of studying, I and all the other students really wanted to have a sense of what we had accomplished, and of the challenges to come. For these reasons we have created a somewhat arbitrary but helpful map of training here at Zen Mountain Monastery, based on a series of paintings from Chinese antiquity known as "The Ox-herding Pictures" or "The Bull Herder Series." The ox-herding pictures illustrate the spiritual development of a student, from the moment they enter the Way until the completion of their training, when they become a master in their own right.

There are several different collections of the ox-herding pictures: a set of eight, a set of twelve, and a set of ten. The set of ten, compiled by Master K'uo-an, is the most commonly used. K'uo-an added a verse and a commentary to each picture to indicate the nature of spiritual practice in that stage. At Zen Mountain Monastery, we adopted K'uo-an's pictures and verses, roughly correlating them to ten stages of training.

Of course, the process could be broken up into any number of steps; there are no distinct transitions, only a sense of interfaces between stages that are essentially quite subtle. Also, at each stage all of the eight areas of training are pursued, and a student's progress may be very rapid in one area but very sluggish in another. So, it's not as clear cut as we might like it to be. However, applying the ten ox-herding pictures to the dynamics of training allows us to talk about it and gives us some sense of how the whole process works.

If you were to say to someone practicing Zen outside of Zen Mountain Monastery, either in the United States or in Asia "I'm in the fourth stage of training; what stage are you in?" they wouldn't know what you were referring to. If you asked them how they were doing in liturgy practice or body practice, the question wouldn't make any sense to them. The methods that we are talking about are not a universal way of doing practice, but are particular to the Mountains and Rivers Order and Zen Mountain Monastery.

It seems to me that people train better when they are informed about and clear on what they are doing, especially when the maps are balanced with mysteries. We continue to reserve plenty of space in Zen training for the great mysteries, and that balance is persistently at work in the teacher-student relationship. Although students may have a sense of where they are in terms of the stages of training, they really don't have a sense of where they are in terms of approval from the teacher regarding their understanding of the koans and the teachings. Here, the empowerment has to come from within.

STAGE ONE

The first stage of training has to do with the search, with the emergence of questions and the entering onto the path. There are all kinds of searches and all kinds of questions. Sometimes the search is for psychological well-being,

1. The Search for the Ox

In the pastures of the world,
I endlessly push aside the tall grasses in search of the ox.
Following unnamed rivers,
lost upon the interpenetrating paths of distant mountains,
My strength failing and my vitality exhausted,
I cannot find the ox.
I only hear the locusts chirring through the forests at night.

sometimes for physical well-being, and sometimes for spiritual well-being. Many people come to training centers and monasteries seeking something that is not necessarily within the province of what a monastery or training center can provide. Most Zen teachers and Zen centers are not equipped to deal with someone who is troubled by significant psychological tensions and distortions. Common neurosis and anxiety are one thing, deep psychological problems are quite another.

Because it is important to clarify the motivation for entering training, we ask prospective students to meet with the Mountains and Rivers Order Guardian Council. The Guardian Council sees what is moving the person to seek training, and, if what they are looking for is physical or psychological health, will redirect them to somebody that can better help them. Physical and psychological well-being are often by-products of this training, but if they are a student's main goal, there are more appropriate ways to work on them. But if the student is concerned with the ground of being, with fundamental questions of life and death — Who am I? What is truth? What is reality? What is life? What is death? — then they have come to the right place. Those are spiritual questions, and that is what Zen training is specifically designed to deal with. Those who begin Zen practice without an essentially spiritual motivation usually do not last too long in training.

We first try to ascertain that those applying for training are involved in a genuine search. The ox depicted in K'uo-an's pictures represents the true self; thus the search is basically the search for the self, the nature of the self. The search commences the moment one raises the *bodhi mind*. The bodhi mind is the mind of enlightenment, the impulse and the aspiration for enlightenment, the aspiration to realize oneself. By the time students have come to the Monastery hoping to enter into practice, they have already come in touch with the bodhi mind. If they haven't, the encounter with the Guardian Council can bring it to a head. If the bodhi mind has not been raised; if this is not a question of life and death; if, indeed, there is no question, then obviously there is no answer. The question needs to come up if practice is to begin.

Te-shan was a great scholar of the *Diamond Sutra* who lived in China during the T'ang Dynasty. He was very well versed in the sutra and known all over northern China as one of its outstanding commentators. He had heard that in southern China Zen was being touted as a "special transmission outside the scriptures," and was enraged by the idea that one didn't need to know how to read or be acquainted with the scriptures to be able to realize oneself. He traveled south to denounce this seeming heresy.

This was a man who had no questions — he had all the answers. He was filled with the *Diamond Sutra* and felt he understood the teachings frontwards and backwards. There wasn't a part of the sutra he couldn't quote perfectly and elaborate on brilliantly. When he arrived in the southern region he had an encounter with an old woman selling tea by the roadside, who, by chance, happened to be an incognito Zen Master. She questioned him on the *Diamond Sutra:* "In that sutra, it says 'past mind cannot be grasped, future mind cannot be grasped, present mind cannot be grasped.' With which mind will you accept this tea if I offer it to you?" Te-shan, dumbfounded, fell silent, having been thrown into a state of great doubt. Where there had been the solidity of his knowledge and acumen, now opened a dark void. At that point, the search began for him. Before, there were no questions and no quest. He was dead in his expertise.

The old woman teacher revived him, and directed him to a monastery where he could continue to deepen his practice. He went off to study with Lung-t'an, who took his question and brought it into intense focus until, finally, Te-shan broke through it. Prospective students at Zen Mountain Monastery have to address and clarify that same search, that same great doubt, in order to enter into training.

This initial step of entering training is made very conscious here at the Monastery. There is in Zen a long tradition supporting the notion of entry as a "turning point" in spiritual practice, but in recent times, particularly in this country, the mode of entry into Zen training has become generally no different than it is in other religions. If you want to join the local Lutheran church, you become a member by simply paying your dues and attending. Most Zen centers and Zen communities operate the same way. They are membership corporations; you become a member of the corporation by meeting its financial obligations. At Zen Mountain Monastery we use a monastic form in which the association an individual makes with the institution is not as a member but, rather, as a student. This is the same way one enters a Western monastery even to this day. Traditionally, both in the East and the West, there are barriers of entry. In Catholicism, there are long periods of postulancy and novitiate before the final ceremony of ordination.

Here, we have expressed the traditional barrier gate of Zen monasteries with what we call "The Five Barrier Gates." Prior to encountering these gates, one comes into training for a weekend as a provisional student. People who come for the Zen Training Workshop are being trained as if they were students in that there are demands placed on them and challenges presented to them. They are required to follow the rules and the daily schedule of the monastery and to be disciplined in their sitting. They engage in face-to-face teaching. This experience gives them the chance to taste Zen training for themselves and it provides the members of the Guardian Council an opportunity to see how they deal with the role of being a student. If, after the training weekend, they want to become a Mountains and Rivers Order student, they formally present an application to and meet with the Guardian Council.

The next step is *Tangaryo*, an all-day sitting, during which a prospective student can reflect on the commitment being made. Tangaryo is a time to get very clear about what it is that one wants to accomplish, and to make a personal vow to accomplish just that. The Welcoming Ceremony which happens after Tangaryo marks the forming of a bond between teacher and student and involves an exchange in which the student offers a token gift and the teacher pours tea for the student. This is followed by an Entering Ceremony in which the new student is accepted by the sangha. The final step is *shoken*, asking for the teachings. This, too, is essential because until the student is consciously reaching out, the teacher does not respond. Until asking happens, the frame of consciousness that creates Zen mind, beginner's mind, has not yet become activated.

It would be easy to take the process of entry into practice very routinely if this elaborate structure wasn't in place to make it very conscious. We are accustomed to meeting the various requirements involved with everything from getting a driver's license to entering college to getting a job. In general, we don't really look deeply at what it is that we are doing and the importance of each step required. The Mountains and Rivers Order barrier gates of entry are not some sort of blind ritual, but a deliberate part of our training. They involve a raising of one's consciousness and a clarification of what this incredible Dharma journey is about. Once this happens, the groundwork is set for the real practice, the search for the self, to begin.

In the ox-herding series, each of the ten pictures is accompanied by a poem and a comment of Master K'uo-an. About the first picture he writes, "It's only because of separation from my true nature that I fail to find it. In the confusion of the senses I lose even its tracks. Far from home I see many crossroads, but which one is the right one I know not. Greed, fear, good, bad, entangle me." Practice at this stage has to do with letting go, with making oneself empty and receptive and with noticing all of the crossroads. Working with the breath, the student becomes aware of the activity of the mind, its constant chatter and running commentary, and begins to quiet and focus it, finding the center of their being and returning easily again and again to its stillness. When samadhi, single-pointedness of mind, has been developed, we begin to move into the second stage.

Stage Two

During the early phases of practice, many people are seduced by the exotic trappings of the monastic setting — the robes, incense, sounds of bells, feeling of stillness and awe. This novelty and intensity mark a honeymoon period of practice. With time, as the focus of the concentration repeatedly settles on the breath, the external distractions fade away and the real work begins.

In the second stage, the student develops great faith, great doubt, and great determination, the three pillars of sound practice. Some people come into training with this kind of attitude, while others need to bring it up and cultivate it. The grasp of the teachings tends to be very intellectual at this point and the whole thrust of practice has to do with taking that intellectual understanding and making it very personal and intimate. Students begin this process by working on the first koan or by doing *shikantaza*,

2. *Discovering the Footprints*

Along the riverbank under the trees,
I discover footprints.
Even under the fragrant grass I see his prints.
Deep in remote mountains they are found.
These traces can no more be hidden than one's nose,
looking heavenward.

just sitting. These are two techniques that lead to the same place. In engaging them, one is developing trust in oneself and trust in the teacher. There is movement towards the edge of the practice, then a pulling back — a cyclic venture towards the unknown and a retreat back to a safe place. The student tends to be very preoccupied with the practice and it becomes something that is separate from everything else. "My practice" may seem to be rarefied, special, and profound — utterly distinct from washing my face, cooking a meal, or sweeping the floor. This area of "sacred" activity can for awhile serve to create more differentiation than real intimacy.

The second stage is also about orienting oneself. "Along the river bank under the trees, I discover footprints. Even under the fragrant grass, I see his prints. Deep in the remote mountains they are found. These traces can no more be hidden than one's nose looking heavenward." The implication of the second painting is that what we are seeking is already what our life is about, that it is not something outside of our life. In the second stage of training, a little bit of light begins to shine. Things begin to make sense. One starts to see the inter-relationship of liturgy with zazen, to hear what is being said in the Dharma Discourses, and to notice what is going on in the other areas of training. But, still, it is all very much up in the head. A student at this point experiences some grounding in concentration and single-pointedness of mind. The internal dialogue slows down enough so that for short periods of time, during intense stretches of sitting such as during sesshin, one has the experience of "body and mind falling away." In most cases, students themselves are not aware of this experience, but there is good evidence that it has begun to happen, made obvious by changes in their lives, by the way they do things and relate with others. But these shifts are very subtle. They are not dramatic, not a "big deal."

Students studying koans begin in the second stage by working with Mu, which means that they take the concentration that they have developed with the breath and now direct it toward Mu. Mu becomes the bottom-line question. Mu is the distillation of all of those questions regarding the ultimate nature of reality that bring us into spiritual practice. Who am I? What is truth? What is reality? What is life? What is god? All the questions collapse down to one: Mu. What is it? And the wonderful thing about working with Mu, the wonderful thing about working with any of the first koans, is that there is no place to take hold of them. So, the process becomes very frustrating for the student. Other first koans that people work with are "What is the sound of one hand clapping?" or "What is your original face, the face you had before your parents were born?" These koans have the same quality as Mu; they are unapproachable and don't lend themselves to linear, sequential thought. In fact, they are specifically created to short-circuit the whole intellectual process. You can't resolve the question "What is Mu?" by logic or any of the other techniques we usually use in problem solving. Something else needs to happen. It requires more of a quantum leap in intuition than an answer to the question. Resolving the koan is more a state of consciousness than a specific entity.

Some students entering the second stage of training take up the practice of shikantaza, which is often defined as "just sitting," though its simplicity itself is quite a profound and challenging practice. There is no attempt to develop concentration in shikantaza. Concentration involves focusing attention: a thought comes up, you acknowledge it, release it, and come back to the breath. You keep practicing that coming back to the breath, and begin to develop an ability to let go of thoughts and put your mind where you want it. The more you practice, the stronger that power of concentration, joriki, becomes.

In shikantaza, joriki is developed in a totally different, almost opposite, way. In shikantaza, there is no attempt to let go of a thought. You simply watch the thoughts, the flow of thoughts, without analyzing them, judging them, attempting to understand or categorize them. You are just aware of them. The one thing necessary to the practice of shikantaza is awareness. Thoughts can't persist when there is attentiveness given to them. When you really put your energy into them, and the illumination of your awareness shines on them, thoughts tend to slowly disintegrate by themselves. They begin to break up and dissipate. They don't last. Little by little, the thoughts begin to slow down, finally reaching a point where they disappear. And when the thought disappears, the thinker disappears, because the thought and the thinker are two parts of the same reality; they are interdependent entities; one can not exist without the other. When that happens, what you are experiencing is samadhi.

When you are working on the koan Mu, you let go of thoughts and bring yourself back to Mu, until finally you are just Mu; with the whole body and mind, Mu. Mu fills the whole universe, and that's the same experience of body and mind fallen away that can happen in shikantaza. The thinker disappears — there's just Mu. In fully embracing either of these two very different techniques, one ends up arriving at the same place, in one case through the development of concentration, in the other through bringing awareness to the flow of thoughts.

A student practicing shikantaza, instead of working on a koan, is studying Dogen Zenji's *Shobogenzo*; more specifically, they are reading the chapter entitled "Fukanzazengi." I then use "Fukanzazengi" in dokusan to keep them from getting too comfortable in their sitting, because shikantaza can very easily become a place to hide, a refuge of quietism. Excerpts from the *Shobogenzo* take the place of koans in the face-to-face study throughout the ten stages of training for those practicing shikantaza. I use the *Shobogenzo* — and there are different aspects of it that are covered in each of the stages — to "poke" at the student and keep his or her practice alive, vital, hopping.

In determining whether a student might do better to take up koans or shikantaza, I consider individual personalities. I tend to direct people who are intellectually aggressive towards koans. It is a good way to cool the assertiveness, to undermine and dismantle the whole intellectual matrix, while harnessing the energy of inquisitiveness and activating intuition. For students who are basically more gentle and have unwavering faith, shikantaza seems to work best. They just trust the whole process. Koans work well with those who have deep doubt. But if somebody who is basically filled with faith and not so aggressive wants to work on koans, I let them. I avoid, at all costs, telling people what to do. That creates the guru syndrome, and that is not a role for a teacher in Zen. So, I try to find out what a student wants, and that's what I encourage him or her to do.

The training in the second stage is also about patience and determination. Frequently, people enter practice with expectations of a certain breakthrough, conditioned by the fast pace, quick solutions, and immediate gratification style of their lives. The work with Mu, the work on the early phases of shikantaza, can both take years. People somehow think that they need to accomplish themselves overnight, that if they struggle with Mu for more than six months, they are spiritual failures. One of my students had been practicing in Chicago and, before arriving at Zen Mountain Monastery, his teacher gave him Mu as practice. He had been studying with me for about three years when he happened to go to California on a job assignment. While he was there, he decided to do a sesshin with my teacher. He began the sesshin and went to the first dokusan. He told Roshi that he was my student and that he was working on Mu. My teacher said, "How long have you been working on Mu?" And he said, "Three years." And my teacher immediately rang the bell, ending the dokusan. He didn't even want to talk to him. Three years? You haven't even started. Go away…

Working with Mu, you get to see what separates you from Mu. To see Mu is to be Mu with the whole body and mind, and if there is something that you're attached to, something that is preventing you from giving your whole body and mind to Mu, then you've got to deal with that and let it go. Whatever you're holding on to separates you from Mu. Mostly it's just trivial, scattered thoughts and habitual patterns of entertaining and sustaining yourself. But if you are in the middle of a crisis or something important has come up, that needs to be processed exhaustively. Sometimes it is anger, sometimes fear, sometimes grief or despair. While you are developing concentration or working with Mu, it is very easy to suppress conflicts and feelings. There are students who are stuck on Mu like a boiler ready to explode, all the while busily pushing away their pain in a desperate attempt at control. At such times, I may suggest that a student change their practice to shikantaza in order to open up their perspective and settle into choiceless awareness. Such a shift in one's way of training may be temporary or permanent. This practice is not fixed and it is definitely not about suppression. It is about realizing the inherent freedom that is the birthright of each one of us.

STAGE THREE

Stage three is described by K'uo-an as *perceiving the ox*: "I hear the song of the nightingale. The sun is warm, the

3. Perceiving the Ox

I hear the song of the nightingale.
The sun is warm, the wind is mild,
willows are green along the shore —
Here no ox can hide!
What artist can draw that massive head, those majestic horns?

wind is mild, the willows are green along the shore. Here, no ox can hide. What artist can draw that massive head, those majestic horns?" Different teachers deal differently with the spiritual experience we use to mark the beginning of the third stage. We consider the third stage as a breakthrough. Other teachers, like Yasutani Roshi, did not confirm kensho or seeing the nature of the self until what we, at Zen Mountain Monastery, would consider the fourth stage.

Where the third stage is *seeing the ox*, the fourth stage is *catching the ox*. In getting that first glimpse of the ox, it is not quite clear what it is that one is seeing. One sees an animal across the field, in the woods, and perhaps is clear that there is this white, huge, four-legged beast. It could be a white horse. It could be a white moose. It might not be an ox. Or, it might be an ox. One has a general sense of what one is looking at, but cannot swear that they really saw it. That is the typical breakthrough that most people get in the third stage, when they pass through Mu. Usually, this happens in a brief moment of deep samadhi, and in order for it to occur, the six senses have to merge. There is "no eye, ear, nose, tongue, body, and mind." For a very short period of time, the self is forgotten. Sometimes this has to recur several times before there is enough clarity for the student to pass through the whole battery of test questions on Mu. There are various ways of seeing and all kinds of depths of intimacy in "being Mu." The fact is that one does not clearly experience Mu until the seventh or eighth stage of training. After the first glimpse, people very quickly latch onto it, make an idea out of it, grasp it and strangle it. That's not it. That misses it.

Seeing Mu is followed by a series of one hundred miscellaneous koans, checking points, and capping phrases, specifically designed to clarify what the student has seen. These koans make up most of the work in the third stage, which can take any length of time, but often lasts one to three years. It depends on the student and how much time they dedicate to their practice with the one hundred koans. The student is essentially approaching Mu from all the various angles. When you look back at it years later, you realize that all you were doing during this stage was Mu in one hundred different ways.

In shikantaza, the first insights that came out of the experience of body and mind falling away start to permeate one's everyday activities. These activities, engaged in a fresh, new way, verify the practice. In other words, one begins to practice everyday activities the way one practices shikantaza — just sitting, just walking, just picking weeds, just chopping carrots. The student is also working with the "Makahanya Haramitsu" fascicle of the *Shobogenzo*, "Accomplishing the Buddha's Great Wisdom."

By the end of the third stage, the one hundred miscellaneous koans are completed. These koans, which are fragments of more complicated koans from more advanced stages of training, serve at this point to further elucidate the nature of the self. In the process of engaging them, students develop an approach of their own for working with koans, and begin to see how the koans function in their life. When a koan is particularly significant or relevant for a student, the student will usually get stuck on it for a while. As the same theme comes up again and again in different forms over the ensuing years of training, the student has repeated opportunities to work with and through it. For example, a student who is preoccupied with death will falter immediately with the test questions on Mu. Then, within the one hundred koans, every time there is a koan that has some relationship to death, they will stick again. It becomes almost predictable. The patterns emerge very early and they give the teacher a chance to work with these important issues throughout the whole koan system. When the time is appropriate and the student's state of mind is ripe, these barriers become an opportunity for powerful teaching.

STAGE FOUR

In the fourth stage of training, the koan collection *Mumonkan: The Gateless Gate*, is used for koan study. We take up the main case, the commentary on it by Master Wu-men, and his verse, treating each as a koan. The student really begins to struggle with the intricacies of koans and with how to use *jakugo*, or "capping phrases," to create appreciatory verses that reflect their insight into the koans. Students practicing shikantaza work with "Genjokoan," a chapter of the *Shobogenzo* specifically emphasizing koans of everyday life. I also skip back and forth in the *Shobogenzo*, introducing whichever section seems most appropriate, and closely related, to the questions that are arising in the student's life. The fascicles continue to activate and to open up the process of inquiry in the student's life and practice.

I adapt the practice to the student's direction of questioning, the same way my teacher worked with me. When I first arrived to study with my teacher, I already had been doing koan study for a couple of years and was moving along. He wanted to switch me to another koan system, which meant starting at the beginning. He handed me the list of koans that I would be working on and I looked at it and said, "This is ridiculous. I don't want to do this." I threw it back to him. If the positions had been reversed, I would have kicked me out. He said, "It is not ridiculous. What do you want to do?" And I said, "Shikantaza." He said, "Okay, do shikantaza." So, I started doing shikantaza, and one day, after he gave a discourse on "Genjokoan," I went to dokusan and said, "You know,

4. Catching the Ox

I seize him with a terrific struggle.
His great will and power are inexhaustible.
He charges to the high plateau far above the cloud-mists,
Or in an impenetrable ravine he stands.

Roshi, in that lecture, you said so and so. Does that mean such and such?" My question transformed itself into a koan. He said, "Work on it." I came back and presented it, and he said, "Good; now how about this one?" I ended up doing "Genjokoan," line by line, as a series of koans. I realized years later that the koans I did not initially want to do, I had ended up doing through the "Genjokoan." I ended up getting the same kind of information and experience. After "Genjokoan," I said, "I'd like to go back to the koan study again." And he said, "Okay," and we went back to the koans that I initially threw away.

In the fourth stage a student begins to get a rudimentary grasp of the nature of the self, yet it is still difficult to get it to manifest it in one's life. You know what you should be doing, you know what is right, but that is not what you do. You often, in fact, do exactly the opposite. In the poem that describes this stage, K'uo-an says, "I seize him with a great and terrific struggle, his great will and power are inexhaustible." That's the ego. "He charges to the high plateaus far above the cloud mists, or in an impenetrable ravine he stands." In the comment, K'uo-an adds, "He dwelt in the forest a long time, but I caught him today. Infatuation for scenery interferes with his direction. Longing for sweeter grass, he wanders away. His mind is still stubborn and unbridled. If I wish him to submit, I must raise my whip." This is a tremendous and all pervasive struggle, the period of the training when you are beginning to bring the habits developed over a lifetime into accord with your emerging understanding. This is the start of the actualization of your insights. And it continues forever. Realization followed by actualization, insight becoming action.

Somewhere in the fourth or fifth stage, the student is usually ready to become a *shuso*, to make the transition from a junior to a senior practitioner. The process of transition is the same for both lay students and monks. A vital aspect of being a shuso is to become a head seminarian or a head monk during Ango, a ninety-day, intensified training period, and to be the model and inspiration for practice to the community during that time. Being shuso is a rite of passage and a time of very vigorous practice. The shuso can go to dokusan every day during the regular schedule, a couple of times a day during sesshin, and has extensive opportunity to develop a very intimate relationship with the teacher. By the time a student has become shuso, he or she has already done most of the major zendo training positions and is ready to monitor the zendo. As part of the Ango training, the shuso gives a first senior's talk, and then their understanding is challenged by the sangha in formal Dharma Combat. This is the first time they are tested outside of the dokusan room, not by the teacher but by their peers. The passage from the junior to the senior position brings the student and the sangha together. It roughly marks the completion of the first third of the student's development, not in terms of years, but in individualized training that needs to be absorbed.

STAGE FIVE

The fifth stage involves *taming the ox*. The pointer says, "The whip and the rope are still necessary, else he might stray off down some dusty road. Being well-trained, he becomes naturally gentle. When unfettered, he obeys his master." The comment on this stage is, "When one thought arises, another thought follows. When the first thought springs from enlightenment, all subsequent thoughts are true. Through delusion, one makes everything untrue. Delusion is not caused by objectivity. It's the result of subjectivity. Hold the nose-ring tight and do not allow

5. Taming the Ox

The whip and rope are necessary,
Else he might stray off down some dusty road.
Being well trained, he becomes naturally gentle.
Then, unfettered, he obeys his master.

even a doubt." Your training has advanced to a point where you are pretty clear on the natural order of things, how you fit into the total scheme, how your mind works, how your habit patterns affect your life, what the trigger points are that bring up anger or fear. You see clearly, but you still remain relatively powerless to do anything about your conditioned, automatic responses. Even though you know why you're getting irritated with people, you still get wrapped up in anger and act on it blindly.

The taming process is the persistent transformation of your theoretical knowledge into an actual, living fact, the experience of your life. "The whip and the rope are necessary" points to the discipline you depend on, the attention you need to apply at all times. You use everyday circumstances to see where your buttons are and how you slip into the reactive, habitual mode of being. You use your practice of awareness to open up the possibility of living more harmoniously. The whole practice is gradually beginning to come together and is less of a struggle. But there is still the nose-ring, the need for discipline to enable one to actualize what is realized.

In a sense, the description of the movement from realization to actualization applies at every stage in the training after the original breakthrough. Every step along the way, every year of practice, I would say to myself, "This is it. I've got it." And then, two weeks later, "Now this is *really* it. Now I've got it." And on and on and on and on, continual revelations. Because what is happening is that everything is getting clearer and clearer. And how clear is clear? It's endless. It continues. There's no edge to it.

Students doing koan study at the fifth stage are working on the hundred cases of the *Blue Cliff Record*. Here, there are more koans concerned with relative perspective and differentiation, that point to how to avoid getting stuck in the one-sided, absolutist view of the nature of reality. The

Blue Cliff Record is a koan collection favored by the Rinzai tradition, and the koans in it are very vigorous and direct.

STAGE SIX

The sixth stage is where wisdom really begins to manifest itself in one's life. The struggle is almost over. It happens with ease now. What you understand and what you are doing become more in harmony. "Mounting the ox, slowly I return homeward. The voice of my flute intones through the evening. Measuring with handbeats the pulsating harmony, I direct the endless rhythm. Whoever hears this melody will join me." The three poisons — greed, anger, and ignorance — are being increasingly manifested as the three virtues of compassion, wisdom, and enlightenment. The comment on this stage is, "The struggle is over. Gain and loss are assimilated. I sing the song of the village woodsman, and play the tunes of the children. Astride the ox, I observe the clouds above. Onward I go, no matter who may wish to call me back."

This is the point of no return for most people. Up to this point, students have a tendency to waver in their commitment, with the strength of their practice depending largely upon their individual personality, needs, and motives. But once someone gets this far in seeing their self, it is pretty hard to turn back. It's kind of like being caught in a vortex, and just going on and on, without any sense of how it is happening. It is returning home. The plum has grown on the tree. It is slightly bitter, not ripe yet, not fully mature — you wouldn't want to eat it. What still has to happen is what we call the great death — *Dai Kensho.*

The student is working with the koans from *The Book of Equanimity*, which are full of subtle nuances and multiple, interweaving layers. The bulk of koan study is behind the student after they have completed this. What remains is

6. Riding the Ox Home

Mounting the ox, slowly I return homeward.
The voice of my flute intones through the evening.
Measuring with hand-beats the pulsating harmony,
I direct the endless rhythm.
Whoever hears this melody will join me.

the *Transmission of the Light*, which consists of fifty-two koans, the series of in-house 108 *Koans of the Way of Reality*, the Five Ranks of Tung-shan, and the Precepts koans. To get this far in koan study without being discouraged represents anywhere from five to ten years of diligent practice. Having completed the sixth stage of training, the student makes a transition somewhat similar to becoming shuso in a public demonstration of Dharma encounter with the sangha, and is now recognized by the sangha and by the teacher as having entered another phase of training as an adept, as someone who has really brought their practice to where it is functioning in accordance with their life. That's what *riding the ox home* is about.

STAGE SEVEN

The seventh stage is called reaching home. The ox is transcended, the self is forgotten. This is what Master Linchi calls "the True Person of No Rank." The ox is gone, but the herdsman remains. The comment on this stage is, "All is one, not two. We only make the ox a temporary subject. It is as the relationship of a rabbit in a trap, a fish in a net, as gold in dross or the moon emerging from a cloud. One path of clear light travels throughout endless time." And, "Astride the ox, I reach home. I am serene. The ox too can rest. The dawn has come. In blissful repose within my thatched dwelling, I have abandoned the whip and ropes." When the ego gets out of the way and the self is thoroughly forgotten, compassion manifests itself easily and readily. The practice is now effortless. I try to reassure people that practice doesn't continue being a struggle for the rest of your life. I would never do it if I needed to force myself to do it, or if it were a continuously painful or unhappy experience to sit zazen or to do sesshins. It definitely gets easier and easier as time goes on.

7. The Ox Transcended

Astride the ox, I reach home.
I am serene. The ox too can rest.
The dawn has come. In blissful repose,
Within my thatched dwelling
I have abandoned the whip and ropes.

The student in the seventh stage studies the Five Ranks of Tung-shan, and the enlightenment experiences of the ancestors, beginning with Shakyamuni Buddha and going up to, and including, Dogen's successor, Ejo. These experiences and what triggered them, recorded as koans in *Transmission of the Light*, have to be seen and absorbed by the student so that they not only understand them intellectually, but make the experiences their own. Study of the Five Ranks helps the student to become fluent in the teachings of the integration of absolute and relative that they have received up to that point. They begin to see how the Five Ranks work, not only in terms of absolute and relative, but in terms of the teacher-student relationship, indeed any relationship, and in all of the dualities.

What has evolved and deepened over the course of training is the ability of the student to see the absolute basis of reality, to clarify that perspective, to see how that absolute basis of reality functions in the world of phenomenon, and to make clear how that functioning occurs. Now, the focus turns to the interpenetration of the absolute and the relative.

The Five Ranks emerged out of Hua-yen philosophy, the highest development of Chinese thought, with Tung-shan formalizing them and incorporating them into training as a hallmark of the Soto School. Tung-shan's teaching is so highly regarded that even the Rinzai School uses the Five Ranks as part of their training in what are called the "Goi koans."

Dogen Zenji, the thirteenth-century founder of the Soto School in Japan, in an apparent about-face, said that the Five Ranks and koan study are worthless. But then he proceeded to write the *Shobogenzo*. And when we read the *Shobogenzo* in the context of this training, we find that there are actually over eighty classic koans included in its fascicles, dealt with in a very fresh and extraordinary way — through the principles of the Five Ranks of Tung-shan. Dogen turns the koans inside out, upside down and sideways, presenting his thorough grasp of the teachings of the integration of relative and absolute in a relevant and exciting way.

During the seventh stage the student is getting close to the point where they are preparing to receive the transmission of the Dharma. They have begun to manifest the Dharma in leadership roles and in the training of other students, gradually taking on more and more of that responsibility. A document of "intent" to transmit the Dharma from the teacher to the student marks the transition to "Dharma Holder" and the eighth stage of training.

Stage Eight

In the eighth stage, "Whip, rope, person, ox, all merge in no-thing. This heaven is so vast, no message can stain it. How may a snowflake exist in a raging fire? Here are the footprints of the ancestors." The comment is, "Mediocrity is gone. Mind is clear of limitation. I seek no state of enlightenment, neither do I remain where no enlightenment exists. Since I linger in neither condition, eyes cannot see me. If hundreds of birds strew my path with flowers, such praise would be meaningless." This is *shunyata*, complete falling away of body and mind. Self and other are forgotten.

The eighth stage is where the student works on the 108 *Koans of the Way of Reality*, koans that have evolved right here at the monastery and in the lives of the practitioners. There are 108 koans — prologue, main case, verse, and footnotes — and they deal with issues not usually addressed by the traditional koan system. Just as the koans of antiquity were collected by different masters to train their monks, and teachers selected cases with an eye for their monks' needs, the Zen Mountain Monastery collection of koans functions in the same way for the

8. Both Ox and Self Transcended

Whip, rope, person, and ox — all merge in No Thing.
This heaven is so vast, no message can stain it.
How may a snowflake exist in a raging fire?
Here are the footprints of the ancestors.

contemporary student. These koans deal with the dilemmas that people in the twentieth and twenty-first centuries face in their lives. They deal with problems and issues that arise out of situations that weren't as topical two thousand or five hundred years ago, such as conflicts within families and between sexes, lay practice, war and peace, compassion, moral and ethical teachings, concerns about the environment and ecology. They come from the sutras, from Dogen's *Three-Hundred Koan Shobogenzo* (as distinguished from the fascicle collection), from the Bible and modern literature, from the Dharma Combats that have occurred in our zendo, from the questions that have come out of students' mouths, and from the dialogues that ensued. They tend to pull together and fill in the gaps, creating a very complete koan system, and one that is very relevant to the contemporary, Western practitioner.

At this point in the eighth stage, the first of three parts of the formal transmission process takes place. Over the centuries, in some Zen lineages, all three parts have been condensed, combined, and done within a week. Here at Zen Mountain Monastery we follow the traditional way, the way Master Dogen received the transmission from his teacher Ju-ching. The first part of the transmission confirms the realization of "the great matter," and infers the teacher's seal of approval, affirmation that the student has indeed realized themselves. Kensho and satori are different. One literally means "seeing the nature of the self," and the other is the equivalent of enlightenment. Kensho is not necessarily enlightenment; it is a glimpse, an opening.

STAGE NINE

The ninth stage is called *reaching the source*. K'uo-an's description is "Too many steps have been taken returning to the root and the source. Better to have been blind and

9. *Reaching the Source*

Too many steps have been taken
returning to the root and the source.
Better to have been blind and deaf from the beginning!
Dwelling in one's true abode, unconcerned with and without —
The river flows tranquilly on, and the flowers are red.

deaf from the beginning. Dwelling in one's true abode, unconcerned with and without, the river flows tranquilly on and the flowers are red." And, "From the beginning the truth is clear. Poised in silence, I observe the forms of integration and disintegration. One who is not attached to form, need not be re-formed. The water is emerald. The mountain is indigo, and I see that which is creating, and that which is destroying."

There are three bodies of the Buddha — Dharmakaya, Sambhogakaya, and Nirmanakaya. These three bodies are the last of the three ox-herding pictures, the Dharmakaya being the eighth stage, Sambhogakaya the ninth stage, and Nirmanakaya the tenth stage. Dharmakaya is the absolute basis of reality; its symbol is the Vairochana Buddha. Sambhogakaya Buddha is the body of bliss, or the reward body. And Nirmanakaya is the "bliss bestowing hands," the physical body and the teachings of the Buddha.

By this time the Precepts, which were originally taken on faith at the outset of training, are now a natural manifestation of one's life. They become so integrated with the person that they begin functioning as an aspect of one's very existence. The Three Treasures, the Three Pure Precepts, and the Ten Grave Precepts interpenetrate with each other and become a dynamic matrix of understanding. With the Precepts, you are weaving the Diamond Net of Indra. You begin to see in your everyday life how wisdom and compassion can be brought to life in the world of differentiation.

There are one hundred and twenty koans that deal with the Precepts and their understanding. They need to be understood from the perspective of the Five Ranks of Tung-shan, from the absolute point of view, and from the points of view of the Mahayana, the Hinayana, and the Vajrayana. They have to be grasped in relationship to each other and with respect to time, place, position, and degree of action.

Metaphorically, the student is now ready to "descend the mountain," to come back to the marketplace, to teach. The transmission of the Precepts and the blood lineage is completed at this stage. This is the second part of the formal mind-to-mind transmission between teacher and student.

Differences in the training of monks and lay practitioners exist all the way through the ten stages, but it is in the ninth stage that the paths completely diverge. Monks begin learning the tantric teachings and continue their work with the precept koans, both being aspects of the training that they will use in performing liturgy, officiating at services, ordaining monks, and conducting ceremonies. They are being prepared to function in the capacity of a religious figure, either as temple priests or as abbots of monasteries. A lay practitioner who completes training will become a lay teacher, and will work with their students on self-realization, zazen, and koan study, will do daily liturgy, but will not ordain monks or operate monasteries. Lay teachers will work within the context of a training center, with people who have careers, families, and other directions in their lives.

If someone, upon reaching the ninth stage as a lay practitioner, decides that they want to become a monk, they return to the earlier stages to be exposed to aspects of monk training that they did not engage as lay students. A monk's training as a monk is going on continuously from the moment they are ordained. Not returning to the beginning, when such a shift in training track has taken place, is a mistake, resulting in a monk who does not know anything about what it really means to practice as a monk.

The major difference between my work with a senior monk versus a senior lay practitioner, both of whom have come through the ten stages of training, is due to the fact that I've had the chance to live day in and day out with the monk for ten, fifteen years. In that kind of intensive, intimate setting, a lot more gets covered than meets the mere requirements. A lay practitioner during the same fifteen years of training may do one Ango and five sesshins per year, may even do periods of residency, but there is not that on-going everyday encounter. The intimacy of the teacher-student relationship, therefore, is just not the same. I really need to know them, to see them in action in various situations, in order to appreciate what I need to cover in the oral teachings. So, if a lay student changes their mind at this point and wants to complete their training as a monk, they are required to spend several years as a junior monk, gradually advancing back up to senior status. Of course, they would probably proceed rather rapidly; nevertheless, it is vital that they experience that part of a monk's training.

STAGE TEN

And finally, the tenth stage: *in the world*. K'uo-an's description is that "Barefooted and naked of breast, I mingle with the people of the world. My clothes are ragged and dust-laden and I am ever blissful. I use no magic to extend my life. Now before me, the dead trees become alive." The comment is, "Inside the gate a thousand sages do not know me. The beauty of my garden is invisible. Why should one search for the footprints of the ancestors? I go into the marketplace with my wine bottle, and return home with my staff. I visit the wine shop in the market, and everyone I look upon becomes enlightened."

This is coming back all the way. The plum, which grew to ripeness in the ninth stage, has now fallen of its own accord. The tree released the plum, the plum released the tree. Where it falls, seeds take root and new trees are formed. This is the image of *Nirmanakaya Buddha*, the manifestation of a teacher in the world.

10. In the World

Barefooted and naked of breast,
I mingle with the people of the world.
My clothes are ragged and dust-laden, and I am ever blissful.
I use no magic to extend my life;
Now, before me, the dead trees become alive.

The process of becoming a teacher is gradual. In the eighth stage, the student is kind of an associate teacher, helping, working with, and doing interviews with beginning students, gaining experience in these interactions. In the ninth stage, a monk completes the priestly training and is able to do all of the expected ceremonies. In fact, for some monks, that might be their role in the world — to be the head of a temple and to take care of a congregation, in much the same way that a parish priest does. A lay practitioner in the ninth stage is able to begin working with beginning students. Someone in the ninth stage who has completed the koans and is training others is called a Zen priest in the case of a monk, or a Dharma minister in the case of a lay practitioner. Then in the tenth stage, there is the Dharma transmission, or Dharma sanction in the case of a lay practitioner, which indicates that the student is now able to function as a Zen teacher or a Dharma teacher in their own right.

At this point, the formality has totally disappeared from the teacher-student relationship. At times, there is a reversal of the roles — the teacher becomes the student, the student becomes the teacher. The merging has become complete. There are no longer two separate entities. In a sense, the teacher disappears. Formal training is over. Dharma transmission or Dharma sanction is the final step in formal training, and the student is now totally on their own. They can manifest their life in many different ways, which does not mean necessarily appearing formally as a Zen teacher. The student may reenter the world and just disappear, or may become a parish priest, or may live a hermit's life on the mountainside. But the fact is, their teaching of the Dharma will be manifesting in all circumstances, all the time. It may not happen in the way I have chosen to do it, in a monastery setting with robes and bells; it's up to the new teacher. But even if the teaching is not visible, it is also not possible to hide it or to hold it back.

Lay teachers who become spiritual directors of lay practice centers, or monk teachers who become abbots of monasteries undergo additional training and oral teachings before "ascending the mountain" (in the case of a monk becoming an abbot of a monastery), or before "taking the high seat" (in the case of a lay practitioner becoming a spiritual director of a center).

The real quality of the tenth ox-herding picture is present in the first picture: beginner's mind. That's what it's all about. It's a circle that recurs endlessly. That innocent mind — the naivete, openness and receptivity of the beginner — is the quality developed fully in the process of coming down off the mountain's lofty peak. No trace of enlightenment remains.

This is an incredible practice, an incredible teaching, probably one of the most highly evolved and refined spiritual practices to have come about in all of human history. We are fortunate to have the chance to do it. Thirty years ago that opportunity did not exist for Westerners. When I was struggling with my questions about human consciousness and spirituality, books were not even available, to say nothing about genuine teachers. Going to Asia was possible, but it did not assure that one would be admitted into the monasteries. To find the Dharma in our own country, manifesting in our own language and in forms that are familiar to us, is a very rare and important opportunity, brought to us at no small cost. It took an incredible amount of courage for the Asian teachers to come here, and an equal amount of ingenuity and perseverance to make the teachings accessible.

Now, it is in our hands. What we do with it is entirely up to each one of us. But we should always keep in mind that what we are involved in is not just the personal experience of enlightenment, not just the clarifying of our own life. *We* are the appearance of the Buddhadharma in the West. The implications of what that means have yet to be seen. Arnold Toynbee, the historian, has said that a hundred years from now, when people look back, it is not going to be atomic energy, space travel, computers, or any of the remarkable leaps and achievements we have made as a civilization, but rather an incident that most people are hardly aware of, that will be seen as the most significant advance of the twentieth century. That incident is the transmission of the Buddhadharma from East to West. Each and every Zen practitioner is part of that process.

THE EIGHT GATES

1. The Still Point: *Zazen*

Master Dogen, addressing the assembly, taught:

From time immemorial the mountains have been the dwelling place of the great sages. Wise ones and sages have all made the mountains their own chambers, their own body and mind, and through these wise ones and sages, the mountains have been actualized. However many great sages and wise ones we suppose have assembled in the mountains, ever since they entered the mountains, no one has met a single one of them. There is only the actualization of the life of the mountains; not a single trace of their having entered remains. The countenance of the mountains is completely different when we are in the world gazing off at the mountains than when we are in the mountains meeting the mountains. Our consideration and understanding of the flowing and non-flowing of the mountain should not be the same as the dragon's understanding. Humans and devas reside in their own worlds; other beings may have doubts about this, or again they may not. Therefore, without giving way to our surprise and doubt, we should study the words "mountains flow" with the Buddhas and ancestors. Taking one view, there is flowing; taking another, there is non-flowing. At one time there is flowing, at another non-flowing. If our study is not like this, it is not the true Dharma wheel of the Tathagatha.

Mountains and rivers are the Dharma body of the Buddha, our body, the body of all sentient beings. These mountains and rivers around us right now are a sutra, a revelation of the eternal truth taught by Buddhism. In *The Mountains and Rivers Sutra*, Master Dogen explores what is meant by "the blue mountain walking," "the east mountain moving over water," and the study of "walking forward and walking backward." Walking forward is activity, manifestation in the phenomenal world. Walking backward is stillness, turning inward, the absolute basis of phenomena. It is important in our training to understand that walking forward and walking backward do not oppose each other. "Flowing mountain" is the activity of the mountain; non-flowing is the stillness of the mountain. This particular passage could also be understood as an expression of zazen:

> From time immemorial *zazen* has been the dwelling place of the great sages. Wise ones and sages have all made *zazen* their own chambers, their own body and mind, and through these wise ones and sages, *zazen* has been actualized. However many great sages and wise ones we suppose have entered into *zazen*, ever since they have entered into *zazen*, no one has met a single one of them. There is only the actualization of the life of *zazen*; not a single trace of their having entered remains. The countenance of *zazen* is completely different when we are in the world gazing off at *zazen* than when we are in *zazen* meeting *zazen*. Our consideration and understanding of the activity and non-activity of *zazen* should not be the same as the dragon's understanding. Humans and devas reside in their own worlds; other beings may have doubts about this, or again they may not. Therefore, without giving way to our surprise and doubt, we should study the words "the activity of *zazen*" with the Buddhas and ancestors. Taking one view, there is the activity of *zazen*; taking another, there is the stillness of *zazen*. At one time there is activity, at another time stillness. If our study is not like this, it is not the true *zazen* of the Tathagatha.

Without zazen there is no Zen. Zazen is the manifestation of the ten thousand dharmas, of the Great Way itself. We may study sutras, liturgy, art, body, and mind, but without zazen they remain only the study of sutras, liturgy, art, body, and mind — not yet the study of the Great Way itself. To study face-to-face with a great master, or even with the Buddha himself, remains only study. It is not yet the eyebrow-to-eyebrow, mind-to-mind intimacy of the Way that is realized through zazen. Zazen itself is the miraculous manifestation of supreme enlightenment. As such, all things sacred and secular, all the so-called "dragons and snakes," when encountered through zazen, reveal the marvelous mind of nirvana, the exquisite teaching of formless form, the very body and mind of the Tathagatha. Zazen gives life to the Buddha.

We should realize clearly, however, that zazen is not meditation, contemplation, visualization, or mindfulness. It is not to be found in the mudra, chakra, mantra, or koan. Neither in its stillness nor its functioning, its seated nor its active form, can zazen be said to be meditation. Zazen is not single-pointed mind, no-mind, aware-mind, or trance-mind. It is not revealed in words and letters, and is only transmitted one-to-one, from Buddha to Buddha.

Although the Ten Stages of Zen Mountain Training are but a single leap, one thing, complete in and of itself, it is very difficult to speak of it in that way. Therefore, we resort to stages and gates to help lay out a path that can be followed. The zazen of Stage One practice and the zazen of Stage Ten practice are the same zazen, but Stage One zazen is not Stage Ten zazen. Yet, the zazen of Stage Ten is, indeed, the same as the zazen of Stage One. Do you understand?

In the beginning of our practice, "mountains are mountains and rivers are rivers." They are manifested in the whole phenomenal universe. After much practice, the self is forgotten and "mountains are not mountains and rivers are not rivers." As the practice continues and matures even further, "mountains are again mountains and rivers are again rivers." The absolute and the phenomenal merge. The mountains and rivers of the beginner are not the mountains and rivers of the mature practitioner. However, the mountains and rivers of the mature practitioner are identical with the mountains and rivers of the beginner. Do you see?

"When ordinary beings see it, they are sages. When sages see it, they are ordinary beings." Although we may speak of zazen in terms of counting the breath, following the breath, being the breath, "just sitting," koan introspection, and various other names and descriptions, we should bear in mind that they are just that — descriptions and intellectualizations of zazen — they don't yet reach zazen itself. The truth of zazen is realized eyeball-to-eyeball, face-to-face. It is in this way that we meet not only the master and all the Buddhas and ancestors face-to-face, but ourselves as well.

When zazen is incorrectly understood, it can lead to a suppression or denial of our human experience and can drive us further and further from the realization of the self. To study the Buddha Way is to study the self — and to really study the self is zazen. Zazen means to be intimate with the self. To be intimate with the self is to realize the whole phenomenal universe as the self.

The very first sitting of the rank beginner, whether properly or improperly executed, is at once the complete and perfect manifestation of the zazen of countless Buddhas and ancestors of past, present, and future. From the zazen of countless Buddhas and ancestors, our own zazen emerges. From our own zazen, the zazen of countless Buddhas and ancestors is realized. As a result, we all live the life of Buddha, transcend Buddha, have the mind of Buddha and become Buddha.

The Zen school is based on zazen. Of all the schools of Buddhism, Zen is the one that throughout the ages has maintained zazen as its core. Yet, through the passage of time, the active practice of zazen has too often fallen by the wayside. During a recent visit to Japan, our sangha members were surprised to find that most of the temples we visited did not even have a place for practitioners to sit zazen, and that neither practitioners nor priests engaged in zazen on a daily basis. In our own country the same kind of thing is gradually happening at many Zen centers. I notice as I visit and talk to people from other Zen centers around the country, that little by little the amount of zazen (which during the late 1960's and the 70's was tremendous) has slowly begun to decline, from what was once monthly sesshins to often only two or three sesshins per year. Because it is very difficult to practice zazen without group support, many non-resident practitioners eventually find their own sitting practice dwindling.

Without a strong foundation in zazen, this practice, this life of the Buddha, can never be realized. The teachings transmitted face-to-face become no more than words and descriptions. The heart of the great matter communicated in the sutras becomes the empty recitation of words. Our art practice and body practice are totally meaningless without their basis in zazen. Art practice is not just doing art; every artist does art. Body practice is not just the martial arts; every martial artist does that. It's only when those practices arise out of the heart of zazen that they become the true practice of the Way.

Master Dogen is called "the great teacher of zazen." The center of all he had to say rested with his teaching of *shikantaza*. In his famous "*Fukanzazengi:* The Universal Promotion of the Principles of Zazen," he says:

> Cease from the practice of intellectual understanding, pursuing words and following after speech, and learn the backward step that turns your light inward to illuminate yourself. Body and mind of themselves will drop away and your original face will be manifested. If you want to attain suchness, you should practice suchness without delay. Cease all movements of the conscious mind, the gauging of all thoughts and views. Have no designs on becoming a Buddha. Zazen has nothing whatsoever to do

with sitting or lying down. The zazen I speak of is not learning meditation. It is simply the Dharma Gate of repose and bliss, the practice/realization of total accumulated enlightenment. It is the manifestation of ultimate reality. In addition, the bringing about of enlightenment by the opportunity provided by a finger, a banner, a needle, or a mallet, and the affecting of realization with the aid of a hossu, a fist, a staff, or a shout cannot be fully understood by our human discriminative thinking. Indeed, it cannot be fully known by practicing or realizing supernatural powers either. It must be deportment beyond human hearing and seeing. It is not a principle that is prior to our knowledge and perception. Thus, intelligence or lack of it does not matter. Between the dull and the sharp-witted there are no distinctions. If you concentrate your efforts single-mindedly, that in itself is negotiating the Way. Practice/realization is naturally undefiled. Going forward in practice becomes a matter of everyday affairs.

Zazen is not a means to enlightenment; zazen is the complete action of the Buddha himself. Zazen itself is pure and natural enlightenment. This is the basis of Master Dogen's teachings: practice and enlightenment are one. It is very easy for us to take for granted this simple practice we call zazen. It is very easy to sit there thinking that counting the breath, following the breath, or penetrating a koan is what zazen is all about. But zazen is much more than that. Even beginners in their first moments of sitting are manifesting the life of the Buddha in their zazen. Having "raised the Bodhi mind," to place yourself in the posture of zazen with the mind of enlightenment is in itself the manifestation of the life of the Buddha.

With our zazen we build confidence day by day. The more we study the self, the more clearly we see the self and the more confidence we develop in ourself. The more confidence we develop in ourself, the more intimacy with the self results. To really be intimate with the self is to be intimate with the whole universe. To really be intimate with the self is the falling away of body and mind. That's what Master Dogen means when he says, "To study the Buddha way is to study the self. To study the self is to forget the self, and to forget the self is to be enlightened by the ten thousand things." We realize that the separation between self and other never existed; that it was a concept, a way of using the mind, that resulted in a deluded idea of what the universe is. "To be enlightened by the ten thousand things" is to *be* the ten thousand things. "To be enlightened by the ten thousand things" means "to cast off body and mind of self and others; no trace of enlightenment remains and this traceless enlightenment continues endlessly."

When we sit zazen we build *joriki*, the power of zazen. But the power of that joriki is directly related to the intensity of our sitting. When we stop sitting and stop creating joriki, our mind drifts back to the scattered state. When we resume sitting and again collect our energies, we again begin to build joriki, the power that effects the breakthrough necessary to experience for ourselves the nature of reality. But even before that breakthrough is realized, zazen is the manifestation of that reality, the manifestation of the enlightenment of the Buddha. In his chapter in *Shobogenzo* called "*Zammai Ozammai*: The King of All Samadhis," Master Dogen says:

Know that the world of zazen is far different than any other realm. At the precise moment of sitting zazen, examine whether or not time permeates the vertical and horizontal (all of space). And consider the nature of zazen — is it different from normal activity? Is it a highly vigorous state? Is it thinking or non-thinking? Action or non-action? Is zazen only the full lotus posture or does it exist in the body and the mind? Or, does it transcend body and mind? We must examine such various standpoints. The goal is to have a full lotus posture of your body and a full lotus posture in your mind. You must have a full lotus posture in the state where body and mind have fallen away.

There are many aspects to zazen. Between the beginning stages of counting the breath and the very advanced stages of deep samadhi there is no gap. In a total integration of the absolute and relative, the development of joriki and the manifestation of *anuttara-samyaksambodhi* are the same activity of the Buddha. Yet when we really look at it, we see that unless we use great determination to maintain, polish, and deepen the zazen mind, it slowly begins to decay and fall away. If we don't transmit zazen, we don't transmit the Buddhadharma, and sooner or later, without zazen, this incredible Dharma will be extinguished. Each time we sit, we manifest the supreme enlightenment of the Buddha in our own life. Each time we strengthen our sitting, we enable the power of that zazen to reach into all of the activities of our life — our walking and working, our laughing and dancing, our eating and crying. That's what practice is about.

Everything we need to know we already have, but unless we uncover it and make it our own, it is of no use to us. No one can do it for us. No one can give it to us. Not one of the Buddhas or ancestors could do that — all they could do is point. The responsibility ultimately is ours. That is what our practice is about. That is why morning, noon, and night we take the posture of zazen. That is why everything we do — all of our 24-hours-a-day activity — is done with zazen mind. Zazen is our walking, our study, our liturgy, our face-to-face teaching, our work, sleeping, resting, and reading. From the depths of the stillness we reach on our cushion, it radiates into the ten directions, reaching everywhere. But unless we find that depth in our sitting, it can't reach out and touch all the activities of our lives.

In the Great Way of the Buddhas and ancestors handed down from generation to generation to this time and this place, there is a single supreme teaching that forms its center, and that is the practice of zazen. Zazen continues endlessly. In zazen there is not the smallest distinction or distance between raising the bodhi mind (the aspiration for enlightenment), practice, enlightenment itself, and nirvana. Zazen is a continuum that transcends time and space, being and non-being. It is pure and undefiled. Its virtue maintains and nourishes self and others. It fills heaven and earth and affects everything with its virtue. It gives life to the koan, the sutra, the liturgy. It is the creative force, the body and mind manifested as the activity of the universe itself. And although this is so, some may realize it and some may not.

By far the most important thing any of us can do is to really make contact with zazen. Get to the heart of it, the root of what it is about, of what practice actually is, so that you know it is with you for the rest of your life — just as you know that each day for the rest of your life you will drink and eat and brush your teeth and wash your face. Zazen is an essential part of our human life. It keeps us connected with our humanity, with who we are and what our life is. It is *that* important. Without it we begin to stray aimlessly. We begin looking for things outside ourselves. We begin "putting a head on top of the one we already have." All along, each one of us is perfect and complete, lacking nothing, but unless we see that, it is of no value to us. The only way to see it is through the Dharma gate of liberation: zazen. It is the gateway, the absolute heart of our practice.

Whether you accomplish yourself or not, whether you realize yourself or not, whether you continue as a Zen student or not — all of this is irrelevant so long as you maintain zazen. As long as the practice of zazen is alive in your life, the life and the realization of the Buddha are manifesting in your life whether you realize it or not. So please, don't take the practice of zazen lightly. It is by far the most important thing we will ever encounter in our lives. Take advantage of it, nourish it — it is a precious gift.

2. MOUNTAIN LIGHT:
ZEN STUDY

Once all of our conditioning is stripped away, the true self is as clear as the brilliant sun. Underneath the layers and layers of conditioning accumulated over the course of a lifetime is a Buddha whose light shines throughout the whole universe. Inside the ego shell of conditioning, a glimmer of that light is actually what brings us to practice to begin with. It is the *bodhicitta*, the bodhi mind, the mind that says it doesn't make sense that there should be all this pain and suffering, or that it should be so difficult to just be ourselves the way a tree can just be a tree or a dog can just be a dog. We humans seem to have a complicated time with just simply being human. We fight with each other, kill each other; we bang heads all the time, even with the ones we love.

It is that ego shell separating us from everything that causes the problem. It is a shell we ourselves have created and called the self. And the fact is that it doesn't exist, except in our mind. We keep everything we consider "me" stuffed inside it, and everything we consider the rest of the universe outside of it. The process of zazen erases that shell. It's not very dramatic, but it gradually wears the shell down. Little by little the shell gets thinner and thinner, becoming translucent, until the light inside begins to be seen shining through. At the same time, the light that pervades the whole universe shines in. Inside and outside almost touch. As zazen continues, the sitting gets deeper, and then the shell opens. At that moment there never was an inside and an outside, but just the light.

We construct the reality that we call self. We construct it by the way we combine and use the organs of perception, the objects of perception, and consciousness. These three being interdependent, when any one — the organ, the object, or consciousness — falls away, then body and mind fall away. Since the self we've constructed, the ego shell, is the problem, or barrier, we must become it and realize the self. To realize that the barrier is the self is to realize the self. The barrier then becomes you, you become the barrier, and there is nothing else. This is the self teaching the self; this is the self realizing the self.

The barrier teaches the self, pain teaches the self, the self teaches the pain. This is what Dogen is talking about in the following passage from *The Mountains and Rivers Sutra*:

> Since ancient times, wise ones and sages have lived by the water. When they live by the water, they catch fish, or they catch humans, or they catch the Way. These are all traditional water styles and, going further, they must be catching the self, catching the hook, being caught by the hook, and being caught by the Way. In ancient times when Ch'uan-tzu suddenly left Yueh-shan and went to live on the river, he caught the sage of the Flower-in-River. Isn't this catching fish? Isn't it catching humans? Catching water? Is it not catching himself? That someone could see Ch'uan-tzu is because he is Ch'uan-tzu. Ch'uan-tzu teaching someone is his meeting himself.

A first reading of this probably makes little sense. As we go through it more carefully, we see that Dogen is beckoning us to another perspective, another way of seeing ourselves and the universe. My teacher meeting me is my teacher meeting himself — and it is me meeting myself. Isn't this the Buddha meeting the Buddha? Isn't my teaching you my meeting myself, you meeting yourself, and Buddha seeing himself? We say that to realize oneself is to be intimate with oneself. To be intimate with oneself is Buddha realizing Buddha. That action verifies and actualizes the enlightenment of all the Buddhas in the ten directions: those of the past, the present, and the future. The dualities dissolve — teacher/student, absolute/relative, form/emptiness.

This intimacy is what the whole process of the teacher-student relationship is about. Ultimately, it is the student meeting himself and the teacher meeting himself; the teacher teaching himself, the student teaching himself. Body and mind fall away and there is a merging, the same merging that takes place in the teaching known as the "Five Ranks of Tung-shan."

The first rank of Tung-shan is that of the relative within the absolute. The absolute refers to the absolute basis of reality, the experience of no eye, ear, nose, tongue, body, or mind. The relative within the absolute is the realm of emptiness, deep samadhi. But in that deep samadhi there is no knowing, because when you become the pain, there is no way to know the pain; when you become Mu, there is no way to know Mu. Whenever you become the koan or the barrier, there is no knowing it.

Knowing it, realizing it does not happen until the second rank, the rank of the absolute within the relative. This is the realm of kensho, of realization. When one leaves the realm of emptiness and enters the realm of all kinds of differentiation — right on the edge of that — one realizes what has been experienced.

The third rank is that of coming from within the absolute. This is "now" activity, a synthesis of the absolute and the relative. It is not absolute and it is not relative. This is where compassion begins to come forth, because when you look out at the world you see your face in everything that you see. You see each thing as nothing but this very body and mind. But this is still not complete. Something is missing because there are still the paired opposites of absolute and relative.

And that brings us to the fourth rank, the rank of mutual integration, coming from both the absolute and the relative. This is also the Tenth Stage of training in the Mountains and Rivers Order, as was illustrated earlier in this text with the classic Ox-herding pictures. What was once a young boy looking for the "ox" (the self), is now an old man covered with dirt, finally coming down off the mountain and back into the marketplace. No one can identify whether he is a sage or an ordinary person. Without being recognizable, he manifests the teachings in the world.

But this is still dualistic. Only in the fifth rank is unity attained. In this attainment of unity, there is no trace of enlightenment, no way to discern the absolute or the relative, the teacher or the student. That final rank is also the last stage in the teacher-student relationship. As the student advances in understanding, the distance between teacher and student closes. One image for this is a dot with a circle around it, the dot being the teacher and the circle being the student. Basically what happens is that the circle shrinks and merges with the dot so that they are no longer distinguishable.

In the case of Ch'uan-tzu cited by Dogen, the language is that of the Five Ranks, except that absolute and relative have been replaced with other words; for example, Dogen talks about "catching the hook." In this kind of language, the one who hooks and the thing that is hooked are not two: the hook hooks the hook. And so it can be said of teacher and student.

The specific story referred to by Dogen, in this passage from the sutra, involves Ch'uan-tzu, who studied with Yueh-shan Wei-yen, a teacher from our own lineage. Yueh-shan had other very famous disciples, among them Tao-wu. Ch'uan-tzu was Tao-wu's Dharma brother. During one of the great persecutions of Buddhism during the T'ang Dynasty, around the year 845, Ch'uan-tzu left the temple at Yueh-shan Mountain and went to live along the Flower-in-River, saying that he was good for nothing, but enjoyed the mountains and rivers. He became a boatman and continued to teach in disguise.

Chia-shan, the person "caught" by Ch'uan-tzu in the sutra, was formerly the chief monk of a monastery. One day in the lecture hall a monk had asked him, "What is the Dharmakaya?" Chia-shan replied, "It has no form." The monk asked, "What is the Dharma eye?" Chia-shan said, "It has no crack." On hearing this, Tao-wu, who was visiting in the assembly, burst out laughing in spite of himself. Chia-shan descended from the rostrum and asked Tao-wu why he had laughed. Tao-wu said, "I have a Dharma brother who teaches others in a boat on the Flower-in-River. You should go see him and you're sure to realize it." Tao-wu suggested that Chia-shan change out of his temple clothes and immediately go to the river. Chia-shan put on traveling clothes and made the journey to Flower-in-River to meet Ch'uan-tzu.

Ch'uan-tzu, as soon as he saw Chia-shan coming, said, "Chief monk of an assembly, at what temple do you stay?"

Chia-shan replied, "I stay at no temple, otherwise I wouldn't look like this."

Ch'uan-tzu asked, "You say you do not, but then what do you look like?"

"I am beyond sight, hearing, and consciousness," Chia-shan said.

"Where did you learn that?"

"Beyond sight and hearing."

"Even one phrase of ultimate reality would lose its freedom forever if we were to attach to it. To drop a thousand-foot fishing line means to seek a fish with golden scales." (A fish with golden scales is enlightenment — this is Zen fishing.) "Why don't you say a word?"

Chia-shan was about to open his mouth to respond when Ch'uan-tzu leapt upon him, threw him into the water and held his head under. Ch'uan-tzu then lifted him up, gulping and gasping, and demanded, "Say a word, say a word!" And again, just as Chia-shan opened his mouth to say something, he pushed him under and held him there. The second or third time his head was under, Chia-shan suddenly realized himself.

When he came up, he bowed to his teacher. Ch'uan-tzu said, "You're welcome to the fishing line, but the meaning of 'It ripples no quiet water' is naturally profound." Chia-shan said, "Why do you want to give away the fishing line?"

The fishing line in this case is a symbol of being a teacher; Ch'uan-tzu is handing it over, just as sometimes the kutz, staff, sheppei, or fly whisk are used as symbols and handed over at the time of transmission from teacher to disciple. Here, because the teacher was a boatman, the symbol is the fishing line. "Why do you want to give away the fishing line and hook?" Chia-shan asked. Ch'uan-tzu's answer was, "To fasten a green float to a fishing line and decide whether a fish of golden scales is or is not." That is, to find out if someone has realized it or not. "If you have realized it, say it quickly, tell me quickly, words are wondrous and unspeakable. You can see such a fish only after you've fished out of the sea wave, only after you've gone beyond discrimination." But while Ch'uan-tzu was speaking, Chia-shan covered his ears and began to walk away. At this, Ch'uan-tzu said, "Quite so, quite so."

And so the Dharma was transmitted to Chia-shan. Ch'uan-tzu advised, "Staying on Mount Yueh-shan for thirty years, I clarified this. Now that you have grasped it, you must not live in Castle City or human habitation and cover your traces. Nor should you hide yourself where you leave no trace. You must go to mountain recesses and lead one person or half a person to succeed in the essence of this Dharma, so that it is not extinguished." Realizing Ch'uan-tzu's meaning, Chia-shan made a thankful bow, and departed. At this, Ch'uan-tzu called out "Abbot!" When Chia-shan looked back, Ch'uan-tzu raised an oar, and said, "Try to tell me — I have something more." At that point he jumped out of his boat and disappeared in the water.

Later Chia-shan became a very popular teacher. Dogen says in the *Eiheiji Goroku* collection of his talks:

> Although when Chia-shan was at the other temple he was excellent in discussion, he expounded the teachings to humans and celestials, he was perfect in speech and no one could defeat him in argument, it still wasn't complete. Since he had seen Ch'uan-tzu, he had realized himself, so there was nothing more to be desired. He succeeded in the essence of the Buddha and became the master. You may seek such a man in the world now, we find it impossible — ah, what a shame. Noble Buddhist trainees must know this: first of all, you must have an indestructible bodhi-seeking mind and fix your eyes upon the absolute realm beyond increase and decrease; see how Ch'uan-tzu left a fishing hook. Who could do such a deed?

The transmission of the Dharma from Ch'uan-tzu to Chia-shan, how do you understand it? In the sutra Dogen writes, "In ancient times when Ch'uan-tzu suddenly left Yueh-shan and went to live on the river, he caught the sage of the Flower-in-River." That's Chia-shan. "Isn't this catching fish?" That's enlightenment. "Isn't it catching humans? Catching water? Isn't it catching himself? That someone could see Ch'uan-tzu is because he is Ch'uan-tzu. Ch'uan-tzu's teaching someone is his meeting himself." To see it is to be it. To see the koan is to be the koan. The only way you can see the koan is because you are the koan. The "someone" referred to is Chia-shan, the person who sees Ch'uan-tzu. When Chia-shan sees Ch'uan-tzu, he is Ch'uan-tzu. That is what it means to see. Ch'uan-tzu sees Ch'uan-tzu. Mu sees Mu. The breath breathes itself. There is no one else, no one "other."

Likewise, "Ch'uan-tzu teaching someone is his meeting himself." That means Ch'uan-tzu meets himself, or Chia-shan meets himself, or both. That Ch'uan-tzu teaches Chia-shan is because Ch'uan-tzu is Chia-shan. And the person who is being met here is the true person. The true person is the truth, reality, enlightenment, realization, the ground of being, satori; it is the experience of meeting oneself. That's why I say that to forget the self means to really be intimate with yourself. What is the self?

Zen teaching is called direct pointing, and is one of the eight areas of our training. We call it direct pointing because that is all it can be — pointing. There can be no giving. That is why one realizes oneself. The direct pointing takes many forms: sometimes it is manifested as the koan, sometimes as just a simple exchange between the teacher and the student. But each encounter, from the very beginning, is part of the process of mind-to-mind transmission. Regardless of the form it takes, direct pointing is the mind-to-mind transmission.

The realization of the Buddha was the beginning. One day on Vulture Peak, addressing an assembly of thousands, Buddha held up a flower and blinked his eyes. The only one in the audience that recognized what was happening was Mahakashyapa, who smiled. The Buddha said, "I have the Eye Treasury of the true Dharma, the serene mind of nirvana, the marvelous teaching of formless form. I now hand it over to Mahakashyapa." This is the direct mind-to-mind transmission of the Dharma. It is the same as Buddha's own realization. And what was transmitted from Shakyamuni to Mahakashyapa is exactly the mind-to-mind transmission between Ch'uan-tzu and Chia-shan.

Shakyamuni looked into Mahakashyapa's heart and transmitted the teaching to him. Mahakashyapa intimately received the transmission of Shakyamuni's face, heart, body, and eyes; so that his face is not his own but rather the face of Shakyamuni — direct face-to-face transmission. Just as Shakyamuni looked into the heart of Mahakashyapa, Mahakashyapa looked into the heart of Ananda, and that same face was transmitted. Ananda then passed it on to Shanavasa, and Shanavasa passed it on to the next generation. Generation after generation, the Buddhas and ancestors, together with their disciples, see each other and directly transmit the true teaching face-to-face.

Shakyamuni's realization was the realization that all beings are perfect and complete, lacking nothing. That means each one of us. But if all beings are perfect and complete, lacking nothing, what could he possibly have transmitted to Mahakashyapa? The Buddha said, "It doesn't rely on letters and it's transmitted outside the scriptures. I now give it to Mahakashyapa." The great master Wu-men Hui-k'ai called the incident outrageous. He said, "The yellow-faced Gautama is certainly outrageous. He turns the noble into the lowly. He sells dogflesh advertised as sheepshead." What's he giving away? Then he asks, "If at that time everybody in the assembly had smiled, who would he have given the true Dharma to?" On the other hand, if nobody had smiled, what would have happened to the Dharma?

Ananda, who had been Shakyamuni's attendant for twenty years and had been present at every talk he ever gave, didn't receive the transmission of the all-pervading Dharma; it went to Mahakashyapa. Is it because Kashyapa smiled? Ananda didn't understand, and years later, after the Buddha had died and he was serving as attendant to Mahakashyapa, he asked, "At that time on Vulture Peak when the Buddha transmitted to you the brocade robe, what else did he transmit to you?" He figured something more must have happened; there must be more to it than the brocade robe. What else did you get? What is the secret?

Kashyapa called out, "Ananda!" And Ananda answered, "Yes, sir!" Kashyapa said, "Take down the flagpole," indicating the sermon was over. What was the sermon? "Ananda!" "Yes, master!" Two arrows meeting in mid-air. Ananda didn't see it, however, until Kashyapa said, "Take down the flagpole." At that moment, the Buddha's kesa entered the head of Ananda and the Dharma moved to the next generation. And so it has been throughout the ages, teacher to student. The fifth ancestor knocks on the mortar, the sixth ancestor shakes the sieve, and the Dharma is transmitted from the fifth to the sixth generation.

It sounds kind of crazy. Is that what the transmission of the light is about? Lung-t'an blows out a candle, Te-shan realizes it, the Dharma is transmitted. Someone else breaks his leg in a doorway, the Dharma is transmitted. A pebble hits bamboo, a shout, a hit. Fifteen, twenty years of training, sitting, working, religious practice — it all boils down to that? Is that what the true Dharma, incomparable nirvana, the exquisite teaching of formless form is — holding up a flower and smiling?

Actually, there is nothing to transmit because we already have it all. What happens in the transmission of the Dharma is something solely based on one's own religious experience. It has nothing to do with initiation, inheritance, transfer of any manner, shape, or form. The word "transmission" really doesn't even make sense unless we say that it is the transmission of the untransmittable, or call it teacher-student identification, where the experience of the teacher and that of the student are in complete accord with one another, fundamentally originating in one and the same truth. If you think it is a flower that Shakyamuni held up, you've entirely missed what that incident was about.

Wu-men, in a poem regarding that transmission, said, "A flower is held up and the secret has been revealed. Kashyapa breaks into a smile and the whole assembly is at a loss." The secret, the truth that transcends words and letters — that is what Kashyapa realized. About the transmission of the Dharma to Ananda, Wu-men says, "Elder brother calling out, younger brother replying: the family shame is revealed." What is the family shame? The family shame is that this inexpressible truth, this boundless perfection, is the life of each and every one of us. The calling out and answering is just a verification of that fact, a verification of the realization of that fact. And the interesting thing about realization is that, unlike belief or understanding, it alone is transformative. Realizing transforms us. Realizing penetrates our being in a way that understanding doesn't begin to reach, in a way that belief doesn't touch. There is a definite place for belief and understanding, but it has nothing to do with the transmission of the light.

The family shame is the eternal Spring, the Spring that continues endlessly, that is not subject to climate, to time, to season. Wu-men is speaking of the "It" which never changes through all the ages and places. And of course, that Spring, that "It," is right where we are. We're in the midst of that beautiful Spring day. Day and night we're in the midst of it. Though our pain and suffering may obscure it, though our baggage may cover it, though our greed, anger, and ignorance may hide it, nonetheless it is ever-present in the life of each one of us.

Dogen says, "For example, water flows from many different places to form a river." Many branches of Buddhism flow toward the Dharma. There is a continual inheritance that keeps the lamp of transmission eternally lit. But the transmitters differ only in form, not in essence. Knowing the proper time for transmission is like the mutual pecking of a shell by the mother hen and the baby chick at precisely the same time. Peck peck… tap tap… peck peck… tap tap. If it happens too soon on the part of the mother hen, she cracks open an immature egg, an embryo is born and it dies. If it happens too late, the chick smothers inside the egg. Precisely the right moment — there is no way to predict it. It's different for every person. Just as the teachers differ from generation to generation in form but not in essence, so too do the students differ in form but not in essence.

All of us have the Buddha mind; all of us are perfect and complete, lacking nothing. And for each of us, our conditioning is different, our karma is different, the things we need to work through are different. There is no way that we're going to be the barrier so long as we're holding onto something, because that much holding on, no matter how small it is, separates heaven and earth, teacher and student, self and barrier. So long as there is holding onto something, there is a self; body and mind won't fall away.

We use zazen to make ourselves empty. We just sit and wait for that process of maturation to take place and the moment of breakthrough to happen. The Buddha had to struggle through his demons — why should any of us be exempt? The demons come with different names and different kinds of packaging, but a demon is a demon; and we construct all of them with our mind and the way we use it. The only way to deal with it is to let it come up, to not run away from it, to not suppress it, deny it, or even reject it, but to welcome it, be it — with the whole body and mind. Only then do the fangs and horns drop off, only then does the fire go out — just like that. That which we create, we put an end to. And once all of the baggage is let go of, once we put down the pack and take off the blinders, then the way is clear and undisguised and there is no longer anything that separates us from the ten thousand things.

Somehow we figure that the basic characteristics of the human species are war, pillage, hate, insensitivity to the environment, the capacity to rip each other off. That is all we seem to be if you read the chronicles of our history. There are people who have even tried to justify, anthropologically and psychologically, that violence. But there is a small handful of humans who, for 2,500 years, have been constantly verifying and actualizing the truth of the Buddha nature by realizing it and actualizing it in their lives, generation to generation. And it is *that* inherent characteristic that is the actual birthright of each one of us. It is the thing that lights the fire, that raises the bodhi mind, that brings us to practice. It raises the questions and enables us to endure the unendurable, to engage in one of the most difficult encounters that any of us will ever experience, to encounter the self, a lifetime of ego specifically designed not to be forgotten.

"This is not the time of yin and yang," Wu-men says of this eternal Spring. This is not the time of this and that, of inside and outside, of good and bad, of heaven and earth. The direct pointing is not only all of those exotic things we hear of — the holding up of the flower, or the calling and answering, the pebble hitting the bamboo, Lin-chi's shout, Te-shan's sixty blows, Ch'uan-tzu almost drowning Chia-shan by holding him under the water — it happens moment to moment. The face-to-face teaching comes out of all that we do when we practice. When we practice with a beginner's mind, the ten thousand things also teach. Zazen points, liturgy points, study points, the koan points, work points, the brambles point and the plum blossoms point. That direct pointing is the best we can do.

We're surrounded by It, we're interpenetrated by It, we coexist with It, so how can we talk about It? Where can you stand to talk about It? How can we even point? The finger pointing to the moon is the moon, and the moon is the finger; the finger sees the moon, and the moon sees the finger. The moon realizes moonness, the finger realizes fingerness; they realize each other. There is no way to separate them — except by the way we use our mind, by what we tell ourselves, by what we construct concerning who we are and what our life is.

Dogen says:

> The interdependence between the Buddha and each one of us cannot be measured. We should sit quietly and reflect on this. Through Shakyamuni's face we will reflect his eye in our own. When this occurs, it becomes Buddha's vision, an original face. This transmission has been handed down right up to the present time and has never been broken. This is the meaning of the direct face-to-face transmission. In each generation, every face has been the face of Buddha. And this original face is direct face-to-face transmission. Open the eye, directly transmit through the eye and receive the Dharma through the eye. Find the direct transmission of the face through the face. Direct transmission is giving and receiving of the face. Open the mind. Transmit and receive through the mind. Reveal the body and transmit the body through the body, regardless of the place or the country. The transmission has always been just like this.

It only takes a moment to break through, and it has nothing to do with whether you're a new student or an advanced student. People sometimes ask, "I've been practicing ten years and I haven't seen it; how come that person has done it in eight months?" Who knows? I have no idea. Eight months, one year, five years, three years, two years, twenty years… the point is that unless you're approaching this practice for the simple delight in the practice, you're missing what it's all about. Zazen itself, direct pointing notwithstanding, is enlightenment. And each time we take the Bodhi seat and assume the posture of the seated Buddha, we manifest the life of all of the Buddhas past, present, and future. That light that is our life reaches the whole universe, permeates everywhere, whether we realize it or not.

Dogen wrote a poem one evening while at his mountain retreat at Eihei-ji:

Evening zazen hours advance;
Sleep hasn't come yet.
More and more I realize mountains and rivers
Are good for the efforts of the Way.
Sounds of the river valley enter my ears,
The light of the moon fills my eyes —
Outside of this, not a single thing.

3. OCEANIC STOREHOUSE: ACADEMIC STUDY

In an apparent paradox, Zen literature places a tremendous amount of attention on "no dependence on words and letters." This is actually one of the basic foundations of Zen teaching, tracing itself back to Bodhidharma, who said, "Zen is a special transmission outside the scriptures, with no dependence upon words and letters, a direct pointing to the human mind, and the realization of Buddhahood." Many people through the years have interpreted this to mean that there should be no academic study in Zen. When I was practicing at a Rinzai monastery, the library was always locked. You weren't supposed to go into the library or read anything. Through the centuries, most of the liturgy in Zen training was abandoned and the koans replaced the sutras. But the principle of "no dependence on words and letters" should not be taken to mean abandoning the use of language, but rather to mean mastering its use, not being a victim of it.

Dogen Zenji criticized those Zen Buddhists who cherished only the records of the ancestors — the koan collections — at the sacrifice of the traditional Buddhist scriptures, and opposed the fallacy of negating language entirely. He said:

> Hearing and seeing should not be regarded as being more meritorious than the sutras. It's individuals who deceive themselves: sutras don't deceive. The mind that's in delusion can be moved by a sutra, whereas the mind that's enlightened and free moves the sutra rather than being moved by the sutra. The enlightened mind is free to elucidate and to appropriate the sutras, to use them freely...

When we devote ourselves to the study of the sutras, they truly come forth. The sutras in question are the entire universe — mountains, rivers, the great earth, plants, and trees. They are the self and they are others; they are taking meals and wearing clothes; they are confusion and they are dignity. Following each of them and studying, you will see an infinite number of unheard of sutras appear before you.

Interpreters of the history of Zen tend to overlook the important fact that each teacher functions within a specific cultural context, just as the Buddha did. The Buddha's teaching took place in India 2,500 years ago, when there were many different kinds of religions already in existence, as well as a highly developed philosophy and metaphysics. Buddhism came into being within that matrix. How the Buddha needed to teach was very different from how later teachers in China needed to teach. Many of the teachers in China found they needed to burn the sutras and chop up Buddha images because practitioners had begun to attach to the words and the images in much the same way as often happens in other religions.

All religions have their basis in the mystical experience of a founder. When the founder dies, the disciples collect the words, the teachings of the founder, and those teachings are set down in writing, becoming the sacred texts, the scriptures. After a few generations, it is the scriptures that are being worshiped. Institutions form, a priesthood develops, and the mystical experience itself is completely replaced by the words and ideas that describe it. This is the kind of context that inspires teachers to burn sutras and Buddha images: they have to react to the circumstances of the time in order to reinvest the tradition with life. We are not a Buddhist culture. For us in America, the circumstances of time and place indicate something altogether different. We need to learn to bow, to learn what sutras are about, what liturgy is about. We need to learn the words and ideas that describe reality, as well as to go beyond the words and ideas.

Master Dogen emphasizes in his teaching that there is no distinction between the two. The koan is the sutra; the sutra is the koan. And both sutras and koans can be liberated from the narrow confinement of traditional understanding which views them as nothing but instruments or means. Radically understood, they are no longer means to an end, but means which embody the end. Then, the words and letters, the language and symbols that are the components of sutras and koans have a positive significance in the total scheme of spiritual teaching. The sutras and where the sutras lead are the same reality. The process and the goal, practice and enlightenment, are the same reality.

During Dogen's time, people contended that the koans were correct and the sutras were not. They accepted Shakyamuni's raising the flower on Mount Gridhrakuta, the blinking of the eyes, and the smiling of Mahakashyapa as the true mind-to-mind transmission of the Buddha. They abandoned the study of the sutras, misunderstanding the true nature of the sutras' words. Dogen argued that if the Buddha's words, the words of the sutras, are shallow, then his raising the flower without a word must also be superficial. Dogen said:

> When people say that Buddha's utterances are comprised of mere words, they don't understand the Buddhadharma. The practitioner's daily language should be one with the entire ten quarters of the universe. Their words should be upright, non-dualistic. You should clearly understand that because everyday language is the whole universe, the whole universe is everyday language. We should be able to appropriate words freely in our utterances, making an ocean into a mouth, a mountain into a tongue. This is the daily life of proper language. Therefore, he who covers his mouth and closes his ears, yet can

speak freely and hear everything, is the truly enlightened person who understands the truth of the ten directions of the universe.

There is a famous saying in Zen that "painted cakes do not satisfy hunger." A person reading a description of a wonderful seven-course meal, from appetizer to dessert, is not filled by that meal. The painted cakes are the words and ideas. The usual teaching is that painted cakes can't satisfy hunger, don't reach the truth, can't solve the problem. But Dogen says:

> Examine carefully the pictured Buddhas and the pictured cakes… All are nothing but pictures. Thus viewed, birth and death, coming and going, are pictures without exception. Supreme enlightenment is nothing but a picture. As a rule, in the phenomenal world and the empty sky, there is nothing that is not a picture. If you say that a picture is not real, all things are not real. If all things are not real, Dharma is not real. If Dharma is real, then pictured cakes should be real.

Picture is reality; reality is picture. The non-dual conception of picture and reality is very evident. We create what we call reality with our mind. The object of perception — picture, the organ of perception — eye, and consciousness come together to form that reality. So, a picture of Buddha is Buddha. The word of ancient Buddhas is the whole phenomenal universe. It has nothing to do with the creation of the universe; it *is* the universe itself. It is the rocks and water, the wind, the shout, the raising of the stick, it is the ninety-two fascicles of the *Shobogenzo*.

There are times to say, "Burn the Buddha image," and there are times to say, "Bow to the Buddha image." There are times that the water is wet, and there are times that the water is not wet. There are times that water is not dry; there are times that water is dry. Each time, the statement is in accord with the circumstances; that's what is called "acting according to imperative." That's why Dogen did what he did: his imperative was defined by thirteenth-century Japan. That's why Shakyamuni did what he did: his imperative was defined by what he found 2,500 years ago in India. Our imperative is defined by twentieth-century America — very different. But the principle doesn't change, the truth doesn't change; just the skillful means for realizing it change. We have a very highly-educated sangha who know a hundred thousand times more about the universe than a monk who was visiting Master Ma-tsu knew. Ours is a very different sangha in terms of sophistication and information. But the Way is the Way; that hasn't changed. The apparent paradox of a written teaching in a tradition that cuts beneath words is actually no paradox at all. To realize that is to realize the "Oceanic Storehouse," the total freedom that isn't stuck to words or to silence.

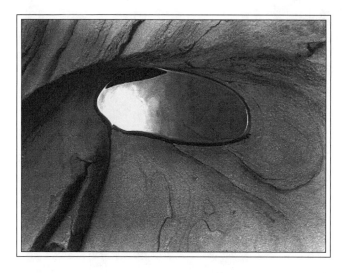

4. MAKING VISIBLE THE INVISIBLE: *LITURGY*

Just as in the arts of painting, poetry, music, and dance, in Zen liturgy we manifest that which is known to us intuitively and subconsciously in the form of a visible, tangible reality. In this way, liturgy tends to make palpable the common experience of a group. There is, however, very little explanation of liturgy generally available. It is rare to see a substantive work on the subject in Buddhism or any of the other major religions. At best, we're given an explanation of the form, usually with little or no insight or understanding as to how the liturgy really functions or what it means. Indeed, liturgy is a very difficult subject to talk about because it is so fundamentally experiential, so intimate, that talking about it tends to move us further and further from the heart of the matter.

Many Americans come from religious traditions in which the experience of liturgy has become no more than a collection of meaningless gestures and rituals. Because it doesn't fit into our scientific reference system, our tendency may be to reject it outright. We seem, in fact, to be a culture with distinctly polarized reactions to liturgy. While at the one end there are those who become very attached to the forms, at the other extreme are those who adamantly reject everything even remotely resembling religious ritual. Yet, in actuality, whether we realize it or not, we are immersed in secular ritual all the time. From the United States Senate to the Marine Corps to baseball fans enjoying a game at the stadium, there is a liturgical identification between the people and the events they are involved in. And, in a way, Zen liturgy is similar to these secular liturgies.

Ritualistic behavior is an integral part of all life — not only the life of human beings, but every kind of life, from bees, wolves, cats, birds, insects, and worms right down to bacteria. Ritual is simply an inherent aspect of social interaction. Part of the problem we have with liturgy in this country comes about because we like to consider ourselves an essentially secular culture while, in fact, there is a theistic supposition underlying the way most of us understand how the universe works. This becomes obvious in how difficult it is for most Americans to recognize sacred ritual or liturgy that does not address a divine being. Put most simply, the question we have to deal with in non-theistic Zen liturgy is, "What is the ritual about if the Buddha is not a god?"

Generally defined, liturgy can be considered an affirmation or restatement of the common experience of a community. In theistic religions liturgy reaffirms one's relationship with God. In Christianity this is expressed through an emphasis on one's relationship with Jesus, while in Judaism there is a focus on reconnecting the individual with the teachings of the Old Testament. In Zen the question of a divine being is not central and, instead, the emphasis is on the ground of being, the Buddha nature, which is not separate from the nature of the self.

All of Zen's rites and rituals are constantly pointing to the same place, to the realization of no separation between the self and the ten thousand things. Zen liturgy is *upaya*, skillful means. Like zazen and all the other areas of our training, it functions as a way of uncovering the truth which is the life of each one of us. Zen study, face-to-face teaching, work practice, academic study, art practice, body practice, the Precepts all point to the same place: the nature of the self, the ground of being itself. Skillful means are necessary because each one of us, just as we are, is already perfect and complete. We lack nothing. What we seek is exactly where we stand. But knowing this doesn't do anything; it is not a matter of knowing. It has to be realized as the functioning of our lives. And for practice to function, for liturgy to function, it must first be wholeheartedly engaged. Practice is always with the whole body and mind. Just imitating the honchos, aping the form — "monkey see, monkey do" — is a dead end. It is like binding oneself without a rope.

A monk asked Master Ta-kuang, "Ch'ang-ch'ing once said, 'He seems to observe reflection and thanksgiving before the meal.' What was the essence of his meaning?" Ta-kuang did a dance. The monk bowed. Ta-kuang asked him, "What have you seen that brings you to bow?" The monk did a dance. Ta-kuang said, "You wild fox spirit!"

The question the monk asks Master Ta-kuang in this koan refers to two earlier incidents, one between Master Chin-niu and his sangha, and a later one involving Master Ch'ang-ch'ing. Every day at lunch time Chin-niu would bring out a steaming pail of rice and place it on the floor in front of the monks. Then he would do a little dance, laugh loudly, and say, "Dear Bodhisattvas" (referring to the monks), "come and take your meal!" Later, a monk asked Master Ch'ang-ch'ing about the meaning of old Master Chin-niu's actions. Ch'ang-ch'ing answered, "He seems to observe reflection and thanksgiving before the meal."

Another monk later picks up on this case and, not understanding Ch'ang-ch'ing's response, asks his teacher, Master Ta-kuang, what it means. In answer, Ta-kuang does a dance. The monk responds with a bow. Ta-kuang then tests the monk to see what he has understood: "What have you seen that you bow?"

The monk does a dance. Ta-kuang then yells at him, calling him a "wild fox spirit."

I ask you today, how do you understand the meaning of Ch'ang-ch'ing's words, "He seems to observe reflection and thanksgiving before the meal?" All of our services in Zen training are an expression of gratitude and thanksgiving. The question is, gratitude to whom or to what?

The first morning service at the Monastery each day is dedicated to Shakyamuni Buddha and expresses our identification with him. Shakyamuni Buddha is not dead — a hall full of Buddhas identify with him. But what does "Buddha" mean? What does "enlightenment" mean? Is enlightenment something that you get or that is given to you? Of course not. This is why we say that there are no Zen teachers and there is nothing to teach, pointing again to the fact that we already have what we seek. This first daily service expresses that wisdom. It is an identification with what we already have — our Buddha nature, the intrinsic enlightenment of each one of us.

The service is also an expression of gratitude for the teachings of the historic Buddha, for the fact that after he realized himself, he didn't just take off for some mountaintop retreat with the attitude, "Well, I got what I was seeking for the last eight years — to Hell with everybody else!" Instead, he stayed in the world for forty-seven years, teaching the unteachable, so that this incredible Dharma could be transmitted mind-to-mind through successive generations from India to China to Japan, and now to America.

Expressing gratitude is transformative, just as transformative as expressing complaint. Imagine an experiment involving two people. One is asked to spend ten minutes each morning and evening expressing gratitude (there is always something to be grateful for), while the other is asked to spend the same amount of time practicing complaining (there is, after all, always something to complain about). One of the subjects is saying things like, "I hate my job. I can't stand this apartment. Why can't I make enough money? My spouse doesn't get along with me. That dog next door never stops barking and I just can't stand this neighborhood." The other is saying things like, "I'm really grateful for the opportunity to work; there are so many people these days who can't even find a job. And I'm sure grateful for my health. What a gorgeous day; I really like this fall breeze." They do this experiment for a year. Guaranteed, at the end of that year the person practicing complaining will have deeply reaffirmed all his negative "stuff" rather than having let it go, while the one practicing gratitude will be a very grateful person. What you practice is what you are; practice and the goal of practice are identical, cause and effect are one reality. Expressing gratitude can, indeed, change our way of seeing ourselves and the world.

The second morning service is dedicated to the lineage of teachers. We chant the names of the Indian, Chinese, and Japanese *Daioshos* ("Great Teachers") from Shakyamuni Buddha down to the present time and place, and express our gratitude to them, because without their dedication to transmitting the Dharma mind-to-mind, this practice would not have survived. What has survived in our liturgy is the Buddhadharma itself, beyond all the ideas and the words that might describe it. The Buddhadharma can only go from human to human, from Buddha to Buddha, from mind to mind. That is why it remains so alive, so vibrant; and that is how it will flow to future generations. It takes on the shape of the container that holds it, adapting itself to time, place, and condition.

If we were practicing "by the book" — by the words and ideas that describe reality rather than by reality itself — Zen training would not have lasted very long, especially in this country. Going by the book would have us practicing something designed 2,500 years ago in an entirely different culture. If I were teaching the same way the Buddha taught, none of you would be sitting here listening to me. And I wouldn't have gone to my teacher to begin with if he had been teaching that way; his teaching would have seemed irrelevant to me — my society, my time, my place, my questions. The historic Buddha didn't have to deal with our kinds of questions. He had never heard of nuclear bombs or ecological destruction, and because most of his students were monks, there were very few questions about marital and sexual relationships, or about raising children. If the teaching does not take the shape of the vessel that contains it, it is dead teaching.

Books contain dead teaching. Live teaching comes from living people and they transmit it to living people. The truth has not changed, the basic questions have not changed, the basic problem has not changed. What has changed is the skillful means by which we come to realize ourselves. In this second morning service we recognize the effort and flexibility of the teachers who have kept the Dharma alive as it made its way to us here on Tremper Mountain.

The third morning service is dedicated to our family heritage, our personal ancestors. To be asked to bow to our parents is a major stumbling block for many American students. "I can't bow to my parents," we say, "I hate them!" The fact is that until we can accept our parents, we can't really accept ourselves. If you haven't made peace with your parents, no matter who or what they are or how they disappointed your expectations, then you can have no real peace with yourself. This identifying with one's own genetic lineage, one's parents and their parents back through successive generations, is an important Buddhist practice. We begin to see how at this time and place the two streams of life come together, the genetic transmission of our family heritage and the mind-to-mind transmission of the Buddha. They come alive in the life of each one of us.

The fourth morning service is a healing service for those who are gravely ill or in need of the sangha's support. In the dedication to the service, one of the lines reads, "Whenever this devoted invocation is sent forth, it is perceived and subtly answered." But who is it that is being invoked? Who is the subtle answerer? Each one of us and the ten thousand things are interdependent, interpenetrating in time and in space. Where are the perceiver and respondent to be found? All of the sutras we chant and all of the dedications that are recited by the *ino* (chant leader) are chock-full of koans; and like all koans, they remain dark to the mind but radiant to the heart. As our practice deepens and our understanding develops, we open more and more to the teaching, and the truth of liturgy reveals itself to us.

In addition to the daily morning services, there are other formal liturgies used at the Monastery, such as the gathas recited before meals and work. These liturgies precede activities that we don't often engage consciously, and provide a transition, a moment of focus to stop and reflect on what we're doing. Every time we receive a meal we consume life; we kill living things in order to sustain our own life. Buddhism does not differentiate between higher and lower life forms — a cabbage is every bit as holy as a cow. Life is life, and we must consume it in order to live. Only when we do this with full awareness can we take complete responsibility for our action. Hence, there is "reflection and thanksgiving before a meal."

Liturgy also addresses and informs the moments of important transition in our lives — birth, marriage, ordination, death — as opportunities for us to reflect on the teaching and to see how it applies to what we're doing. At a funeral ceremony, for example, a poem is addressed to the dead person. Where is the dead person? How could he or she hear it? Who is hearing it? What is it that is born? What is it that dies? Buddhism teaches that life is the unborn and death the unextinguished. What is life? Do you understand?

In the case of marriage, the couple are already united in their own minds, but their union is invisible to others until it is revealed and manifested in the marriage ceremony. A formal Zen marriage ceremony is performed only after the couple have already married one another — only they can marry themselves. It is the same with ordination of monks. The public ceremony isn't done until, by virtue of the student's personal commitment and vows, he or she has already become a monk. The ceremony merely makes it visible to the community so that everyone can then share and participate in the event. There is no magic to be given; the magic is already theirs — and yours. All liturgy can do is render it visible to those who love the monk or the couple who have married. This making visible the invisible is at the heart of the matter.

What does it mean to make visible something which is invisible? Essentially, it means to bring that something into the awareness of the six consciousnesses. Buddhist teaching recognizes six areas of conscious awareness, rather than the five we're familiar with from Western physiology and psychology. In addition to the five organs of perception — eye, ear, nose, tongue, and body (or seeing, hearing, smelling, tasting, and touching) — Buddhism identifies mind itself as an "organ" that perceives. The organ of perception and the object it perceives, together with consciousness, produce what we call reality. So, a thing becomes real (what we call "real") when the organ of perception, its object, and consciousness come together. My eye, the object that it sees, and consciousness combine to form a tangible reality. When you consider mind as one of the organs of perception, the concept of reality expands beyond the boundaries usually accepted in the West. The object of mind is thought; mind, thought, and consciousness thus create a reality. The thought of hitting someone is just as much an action as physically hitting, or expressing the desire to hit, someone. And just as speech and action produce karma, so do our thoughts.

"Making visible" means that we are able to perceive, through these organs of perception, that something is there, though invisible. What is it that is invisible? What is the common experience of the Buddhist community that is restated in our liturgy? What is it that we recreate through the practice of Zen liturgy?

Another way of seeing liturgy is as an expression of mutual identity. In bringing our hands together in gassho, we take an idea and turn it into an action. When you make something an action it becomes clarified and concrete. We gassho before entering the zendo, before accepting food, and as we greet one another; with each gassho we identify with the place, the object, the person. We acknowledge in our action the fact that all the dualities come together to create one reality.

This identification is why Zen services are not considered worship. Worship requires that there be something which is bigger, higher, or beyond ourselves. In a Zen service we identify with the Buddha — we practice the fact that Buddha and I are the same thing, that you and I are the same thing. The teaching in Zen liturgy always comes from the point of view of realization. Nothing is explained. It proceeds as if everyone knew. One Buddha speaks to another Buddha. To hear what is being said we have to shift our way of hearing and abandon our reference system. It has to be seen directly and immediately.

Because of this directness, immediacy, and intimacy, Zen liturgy functions as an empowerment of the self. Suddenly you realize that it all boils down to you, that you are responsible for the entire universe, the whole catastrophe. When no-separation is realized, you can no longer blame, you can no longer be a victim; there is only the master. And that empowerment comes from yourself to yourself. With the wisdom of realization, compassion necessarily arises. Compassion is the actualization of wisdom in the activity of the world. When the self is forgotten, only the ten thousand things remain. Everything is realized as nothing but yourself. Compassion, then, is nothing but taking good care of yourself. If someone falls, you pick them up; if the environment is polluted, you clean it up. It's your world. Intimately and personally taking good care of it is compassion.

Unfortunately, most of us try to understand the intimate experience of liturgy in the same way we understand science or how to drive a car. When that kind of analysis is applied to liturgy, it kills it; it becomes nothing more than the inane babbling of people imitating something they neither realize nor are working to realize. Analysis doesn't reveal what is happening in liturgy. It doesn't free us; instead, it paralyzes us.

Unquestionably, liturgy requires a degree of faith. This whole practice requires faith. From the beginning, a certain amount of faith is necessary because, initially, nothing that we're doing has been verified by our own experience. We practice faith all the time in contexts we don't think of as religious or particularly liturgical. When you lay a ten dollar bill on top of the counter while waiting for your bag of groceries, there is a period of time when you have neither your money nor your groceries, only trust. You get on a bus and pay the fare before you've gotten a ride, trusting that the driver and the bus company will get you where you want to go. We trust our doctors, our lawyers, and our dentists. We trust our partners and our mates. The world works on trust, agreement, and commitment.

The trust that operates in Zen practice, however, is based on faith in yourself, on a feeling you have now, not on something you expect to gain or believe you will receive from others. It is not, "If I have faith, something good will happen." We practice zazen in the faith that we can realize ourselves, but, ultimately, we *must* realize ourselves. It is the same with Zen liturgy. It begins with an act of faith, but as our practice progresses and develops, our understanding of it changes. Evelyn Underhill, in her book *Mysticism*, speaks of the levels of prayer as the eight stages of "orison" or mystical experience. Beginning with the prayer of "petition," she ends the descriptive sequence with the prayer of "union." Similarly, the way of understanding liturgy in the first and second stages of Zen training is very different from how it is understood in the ninth and tenth stages. By the tenth stage, the student's whole life is liturgy.

In thirteenth-century Japan, when the great master Dogen began teaching at Eihei-ji, he found that the practice of liturgy had largely become a meaningless imitation of form. In a radical step to revitalize the training, he taught his monks a new kind of liturgy. He used the everyday, mundane activities of life as sacred liturgy. This is ultimately what Zen practice is about: descending the mountain, manifesting that which has been realized in everything that we do. Zen practice is not an activity that takes place in the world but, rather, the activity of the world itself.

We live in a time and place of incredible moral and ethical disintegration — in politics, government, business, and in religion itself. It is interesting to look at what is going on in this country and question what is behind the problems we are experiencing. We continue to re-elect to political positions people who have been clearly shown guilty of violations of the public trust. It seems insane that this is happening. Some of the most vociferous and well-publicized religious leaders, not only in the right wing of religion but in the left as well, not only in Western religions but the Eastern ones, break their own vows, their own rules. In the business world corruption and deceit seem to be at an all-time high, from individuals cheating a little bit on their income taxes to insider-trading on Wall Street. Suppliers of services rip off their customers; contractors add a little extra sand to the concrete to save on costs. Why does all this happen?

When you really look at it, you begin to understand that what it is about is power — worldly power, not spiritual power. Worldly power has to do with money or position, the ability to control or manipulate people or things. Spiritual power, on the other hand, has to do with realizing yourself. When you realize yourself, the opposite of manipulation happens. Not that people with spiritual power burn money; they don't — that would be stupid. They just don't use it to manipulate and control other people. When no-self is realized, *other* is realized as nothing but the self. That is what it means to be enlightened by the ten thousand things.

Even within religions, that spiritual power hasn't generally become manifest in the personal lives of the people involved. Somehow the teachings that have to do with the spiritual power of religion, whatever religion a person may profess, are rarely developed to the stage where they are actualized in everyday affairs. For me, the key to this actualization is liturgy. The life of a Buddha is what we renew, confirm, and restate in our liturgy.

To confirm and renew means that wherever you are

and whatever your life is, the teachings will manifest. If you are a lawyer, the teachings will manifest in your law practice. If you are a nurse, they will manifest in your nursing. If you are a householder with children, they will manifest in how you raise your kids. And if you are a business person, the teachings will manifest in your business practices. That is the way the teachings of the Buddha are going to reach out into our society. We are only a handful now, but that handful is enough if we practice. When we practice, life is made easier, not more difficult. Practice doesn't bind us, it makes us free. Greed, anger, and ignorance bind us. The teachings free us; or, to put it more accurately, they help us to realize the inherent freedom that is already there and that has been there from the very beginning.

In the koan I cited earlier, a monk asks Ta-kuang the meaning of Ch'ang-ch'ing's words, "He seems to observe reflection and thanksgiving before the meal." Ta-kuang performs a dance. The monk makes a bow. Ta-kuang asks the monk what he has understood, and then the monk also performs a dance. Ta-kuang says, "You fox devil!"

Master Yuan-wu, the compiler of the *Blue Cliff Record*, provided footnotes to help us understand the points being made in this koan. In response to the monk's question about the meaning of Ch'ang-ch'ing's words, the footnote reads, "The light shines again." The light Yuan-wu refers to is the earlier koan in which this question first came up. Commenting on Ta-kuang's dance, Yuan-wu's footnote reads, "Do not deceive the people completely. He acts in the same way as Chin-niu did before." Does the monk act just as Chin-niu did? Is Ta-kuang's dance the same as or different from Chin-niu's dance?

When the monk bows in response to Ta-kuang's dance, the footnote adds, "He too acts this way. He is right, but I fear he has misunderstood." Traditionally, a monk would bow when he understood the teachings, when there had been a communication. But Yuan-wu indicates in the footnote that the monk has misunderstood. How does Yuan-wu know that? Obviously, Ta-kuang also saw that the monk had misunderstood; that is why he questioned him. How is it that the monk misunderstood? Why was his bow not accepted by Ta-kuang? The footnote reads, "Ta-kuang still should press him; it is necessary to be discriminating."

But isn't this practice about oneness? Why is Yuan-wu saying that it is "necessary to be discriminating"? If you think this practice is about oneness, you had better look into the matter very carefully. Oneness is only one side. There is another side; the ten thousand things. We should understand that the ten thousand things, the whole phenomenal universe, *and* its absolute basis, oneness, are not two separate things. They are completely merged. You and I are the same thing *and* I'm not you and you're not me. Both of those statements are true simultaneously.

The monk did a dance in answer to the question of why he bowed. The footnote reads, "He draws a cat according to a model. After all, he misunderstood. He's a fellow playing with a shadow." The reference here to "drawing a cat according to a model" means that the monk is showing no originality whatsoever; he is nothing but a clone with no understanding of his own. In "playing with a shadow," he is not dealing with the thing itself.

Ta-kuang calls the monk a "wild fox spirit." The term "fox" is used here to characterize empty imitation, rather than the craftiness we equate in the West with acting fox-like. Yuan-wu's footnote on this segment of the koan reads, "This kindness is hard to requite. The Zen ancestors transmitted just this." This same insistence on authenticity — this same "You wild fox spirit!" — is what the eighty-six teachers in our lineage have transmitted from mind to mind, generation after generation to this time and place. The whole thing comes down to that. Do you understand?

Did Ta-kuang imitate Chin-niu in doing that dance? Did the monk imitate Ta-kuang? It is really important to see where there is imitation and where there is authenticity and intimacy. What makes many people reject liturgy so vehemently is this same aspect of imitation; so much of it has become a round of empty gestures and motions. People no longer understand what liturgy is about and just don't take the time to find out what is being said. That is how someone can let themselves off with mumbling their way through a Zen service. What is it about? Who is it for? How is it when there is no imitation? How can you tell the difference between a clone and the real thing?

In Jean Genet's play, *The Balcony*, three men go to a brothel every week and play out certain roles with the prostitutes. One pretends to be a general, one a king, and one a bishop. They are all very convincing and powerful in their roles until a revolution takes place. With the assassination of the real king, general, and bishop, the country falls into chaos and the Madame of the brothel is approached for suggestions as to what the country should do. She proposes that these three characters be installed as the real general, bishop, and king, and actually run the country. But when the opportunity is handed to them to take their fantasies into real life and be the very things they had acted out in the brothel, they can't do it. They could only play make-believe.

Somehow, we are able to confuse reality and the make-believe worlds we create. And much of what we create is based on what we have been told as we were growing up. We are each conditioned by our culture, parents, teachers, and peers, and then we proceed to live our entire life out of that conditioning. That conditioning defines who we think we are. All of these authoritative people have told us who we are, so we go on to manifest their predictions. This practice, every bit of it, is about going beyond all of that conditioning, finding out for ourselves who we are, and then living our life in accordance with what we have realized. That is what freedom is about.

In America we usually have a negative reaction to "observing reflection and gratitude." We tend to rebel against the teachings and try to change them to suit our own particular perceptions of what we think they should be, stripping the teachings of their richness by eliminating an important part of the upaya, carefully evolved over centuries of practice. At the other extreme, there are also people who, under the guise of Zen practice, blindly imitate the sounds and forms of the training. This is definitely not what Zen is about. Great faith, great doubt, great determination (the three pillars of real practice) keep that rote imitation from happening. Great doubt, working in dynamic tension with great faith, along with the deep commitment to continue, keep the student's active edge alive. Zen training is neither rebelling nor conforming. What is it then?

All of this upaya, all of the teaching, every aspect of the liturgy, is a secret. It is the secret to world peace, being revealed in the eighty-four thousand subtle gestures that comprise our practice. It is the secret to social transformation, ecological harmony, marriage and relationships; the secret to raising children, dancing, chopping wood and carrying water. The secret is this incredible Dharma dance called life. But it must be danced to be realized. It is not the words that describe it. It is not the ideas we have about it. It is the thing itself. The dance, the bow, the voice. This is not an empty exhibition of form. It is the actualization of the Buddhas and ancestors of the past, present, and future.

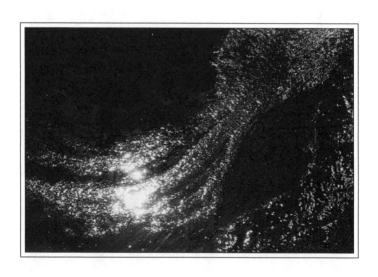

5. THE LIFE OF A BUDDHA: *RIGHT ACTION*

When this Dharma began to take root in this country, there arose a misconception about the role of morality and ethics in the practice of the Buddhadharma. Statements that Zen was beyond morality, or that Zen was amoral were made by distinguished writers such as D.T. Suzuki, and people assumed that this was correct. Nothing can be further from the truth. Enlightenment and morality are one. Enlightenment without morality is not true enlightenment. Morality without enlightenment is not complete morality. Zen is not beyond morality, but a practice that takes place within the world, based on a moral and ethical teaching. That moral and ethical teaching has been handed down with the transmission from generation to generation. Unfortunately, not only was that seed of misconception to find its way into print, but no one bothered to correct it. So, for twenty years it sat there, and although there have been many teachers and many books on Zen, only one even addresses the subject. Somehow, the Dharma of moral and ethical teaching has not been expounded. Somehow, teachers who came from the East and those who have emerged here in the West have shied away from being categorized as moralists.

It is for that reason that the moral and ethical teachings are one of the eight areas of training here at Zen Mountain Monastery. The Buddhist Precepts form one of the most vital areas of practice for the students, regardless of whether they intend to take the vows of a monk or remain lay practitioners. In essence, the Precepts are a definition of the life of a Buddha, of how a Buddha functions in the world. They are how enlightened beings live their lives, relate to other human beings, make moral and ethical decisions, manifest wisdom and compassion in everyday life. At the Monastery, the Precepts are the basis of the rules and guidelines for all residents. For those practicing away from the Monastery, the Precepts provide a way to see how the moral and ethical teachings in Buddhism can come to life in the marketplace, in relationships, in government, business, and ecology. The Precepts are unique among religious ethical teachings in that they are based on the experience of no-self, and that experience makes all the difference in the world.

Here at Zen Mountain Monastery, we regard the intention to practice the Precepts as a very serious commitment. When students want to make the commitment to practice their life in accordance with the Precepts, they may petition to become a Buddhist, and if they meet the requirements, they enter into a week-long special training to study what that commitment really entails. Most other Zen centers have a very different process; at most, all you have to do is ask. If you can pay your dues, you are a student; if you want to be a Buddhist, a ceremony is scheduled. As a result, few people are able to appreciate what it means to really be a student, much less to really practice the Precepts.

It is important that students have a sense of what they are entering into. Because of that, at Zen Mountain Monastery we have established actual barriers that a person has to pass through before formally entering the sangha as a student. Before anyone can enter into an on-going training relationship with the teacher, they are challenged as to whether they are prepared to live the life of a student, to practice like a student. The burden is on prospective students to show what their aspirations and motivations for practice are. In effect, each applicant needs to clarify for themselves whether they are a student; you have to *be* a student before you can be formally accepted as one.

The same is true for receiving the Precepts in the ceremony of *Jukai:* it is not automatic. Before receiving the Precepts here, it is important to have entered the second stage of training. By that time, the vows that are made during Jukai serve to confirm something that has already happened: the Precepts have become part of your life, the commitment and the practice are already functioning. The ceremony merely formalizes that truth.

At the same time, in the beginning, the Precepts are given and received on the basis of faith. At this stage, the student has no personal experience to prove that the Precepts are in fact the definition of the life of a Buddha, of how no-self might function in the world of samsara. All the student has is the teacher's word and the teachings to go by. But ultimately, this whole process, from beginning to end, is something that can only be done by each one of us. There is no teacher on the face of the earth who can actually give you anything, and there is nothing that you need to receive, because each one of us is already complete, and what we seek is not outside ourselves.

Usually it takes several years, and then, somewhere in the middle stages of training, the Precepts begin to really saturate one's life. That ripening, or maturation, is called *prajna*, or wisdom. Wisdom is realizing that there is no self, that the self is empty of any fixed definition. Once you clarify the experience of emptiness, seeing for yourself the significance of that experience of no-self, you begin to see that there are no barriers between self and other. You see that the ten thousand things and this body and mind are one reality, that the self is no other than those ten thousand things. Then wisdom begins to function freely, and faith is no longer necessary. Your experience itself verifies the Precepts. In Zen, we call the activity of wisdom compassion, the actualization of the Precepts.

Towards the tail-end of training, when wisdom has begun to function through the student, the Precepts are actually transmitted formally between teacher and student as part of a process known as *denkai*. At that time, the student demonstrates the actualization of the Precepts by passing through a hundred and twenty koans on the Precepts. By this point, the Precepts are no longer something that has been given from the teacher to the student, but are a manifestation of the student's own life.

The Gatha of Atonement is the first part of the ceremony of receiving the Precepts, and it is also part of most of the other ceremonies we do, whether it be a wedding, a birth celebration, or Fusatsu. The gatha is about intimacy, about "At-one-ment," and comes from the understanding of how cause and effect interpenetrate. In Buddhism the law of cause and effect is called karma. One simple way of saying how karma works is just this: what you do and what happens to you are the same thing. Karma is action, and one of its major characteristics is its power to propagate itself, to continue the chain of cause and effect. This is why in the teachings it is said, "When the first thought springs from delusion, all subsequent thoughts are deluded; when the first thought springs from enlightenment, all subsequent thoughts are enlightened."

The Gatha of Atonement begins, "All evil karma committed by me since of old, because of my beginningless greed, anger, and ignorance..." We identify the causes of evil karma as greed, anger, and ignorance because each springs from the illusion of a separate self. The gatha continues, "Born of my body, mouth, and thought..."

136 The Eight Gates of Zen

These are the ways we create karma. We create karma by what we do with our bodies, by what we say with our words, and also by what we think — all three are equivalent. Just as we noted earlier, an evil thought is just as powerful as an evil physical action. To want to hit somebody in the nose creates karma just as effectively as actually hitting somebody in the nose.

Having identified evil karma and how it is created, we then atone for it, become one with it, take responsibility for it. When you take responsibility for it, you make it your own. And when it is your own, then there is something you can do about it. If you do not take responsibility for it, you are powerless to change it — it is someone else's fault, something else is to blame. You are the victim. Taking responsibility empowers us to free ourselves of the endless cycle of cause and effect. Basically, what the process of atoning does is create the foundation, the readiness, to receive the Precepts.

The first three precepts are vows to take refuge in the Three Treasures — the Buddha, the Dharma, and the Sangha. Buddha is the historical Buddha, but at the same time Buddha is each being, each creation. Dharma is the teaching of the Buddha, but at the same time Dharma is the whole phenomenal universe. And Sangha is the community of practitioners of the Buddha's Dharma, but at the same time Sangha is all sentient beings, animate and inanimate.

To really appreciate what the Three Treasures are requires looking at them from several perspectives. From the perspective called "The One-Bodied Three Treasures," the Buddha treasure is supreme enlightenment, or *anuttara-samyaksambodhi*, the Dharma treasure is pure and undefiled being, and the Sangha treasure is the virtue of harmony. From the perspective called "The Realized Three Treasures," the Buddha treasure is the realization and actualization of *bodhi*, or enlightenment, the Dharma treasure is the realization of the Buddha himself, and the Sangha treasure is to penetrate the Buddhadharma. From the perspective called "The Maintained Three Treasures," the Buddha treasure is "guiding the heavens and guiding people, sometimes appearing in vast emptiness, sometimes appearing in a speck of dust," the Dharma treasure is "revolving in the oceanic storehouse, guiding inanimate things and guiding animate beings," and the Sangha treasure is "being freed from all suffering and liberated from the Three Worlds." It is a very rich and subtle teaching, yet the basis of it is very simple: when we take refuge in the Buddha, the Dharma, and the Sangha, we are identifying with all the Buddhas and teachers. We are making their lives our own life.

Having taken refuge in the Three Treasures, we then receive the Three Pure Precepts: to not create evil, to practice good, and to actualize good for others. The Pure Precepts define the harmony, the natural order, of things. If you eschew evil, practice good, and actualize good for others, you are in harmony with the natural order of all things. Not creating evil is "the abiding place of all Buddhas." Practicing good is "the Dharma of *samyak-sambodhi*, the way of all beings." And to practice good for others is "to transcend the profane and go beyond the holy, to liberate oneself and others." Of course, it is one thing to acknowledge the three Pure Precepts, but how can we practice them? How can we not create evil? How can we practice good? How can we actualize good for others?

The way to do that is shown in the Ten Grave Precepts, which reveal the functioning of the three Pure Precepts. Along with listing each of the precepts, I'll provide excerpts from various teachings that illuminate them.

The first one is *Affirm life; do not kill*. "Life is non-killing. The seed of the Buddha grows continuously. Maintain the wisdom life of Buddha, and do not kill life."

138　The Eight Gates of Zen

The second precept is *Be giving; do not steal.* "The mind and the externals are just thus. The gate of liberation is open."

The third precept is *Honor the body; do not misuse sexuality.* This is usually translated as "do not be greedy," but that translation hides the central issue of this precept. It is about sexuality, about not misusing our sexuality by being self-centered. Aitken Roshi said that, originally, misusing sexuality was defined as "unrighteous lewdness." Practically, what it means is that self-serving sexuality is a misuse. If you are married, adultery is misusing sexuality. Needless to say, rape and child abuse are misusing sexuality. Anything that makes the act or the thought of sex self-serving, disregarding of others, is misusing sexuality. Going to a prostitute, or using sexuality for personal gain, are misuses of sexuality. This is an important precept, and to call it "not being greedy" evades the issue. The opposite of self-serving sexuality is loving sexuality; that is what we need to realize, to manifest in relationship.

The fourth precept is *Manifest truth; do not lie.* "The Dharma wheel unceasingly turns and there is neither excess nor lack. Sweet dew permeates the universe. Gain the essence; gain the truth."

The fifth precept is *Proceed clearly; do not cloud the mind.* This precept has to do with drugs and alcohol. Doing anything that dulls the inherent clarity that is the Buddha mind, the mind of all sentient beings, violates this precept. It can be understood in a very broad sense or it can be seen narrowly. Using intoxicants or drugs whose only purpose is to obscure the clarity of one's mind violates the precept. "In the sphere of the originally pure Dharma, not being ignorant is called the precept of refraining from using intoxicants."

The sixth precept is *See the perfection; do not speak of others' errors and faults.* "In the midst of the Buddhadharma, we are the same way, the same Dharma, the same realization, the same practice. Do not talk of others' errors and faults; do not destroy the Way."

The seventh precept is *Realize self and other as one; do not elevate the self and blame others*. "Buddhas and ancestors realized absolute emptiness and realized the great earth. When the great body is manifested, there is neither inside nor outside. When the Dharma body is manifested, there is not even a single inch of earth to stand on."

The eighth precept is *Be generous; do not be withholding*. "One phrase, one verse: ten thousand forms. One hundred grasses, one Dharma. One realization, all Buddhas. Since the beginning, there has never been anything to withhold."

The ninth precept is *Actualize harmony; do not be angry*. "Self-nature is clear and obvious. In the sphere of the selfless Dharma, not thinking of the self is called the precept of refraining from being angry."

The tenth precept is *Experience the intimacy of things; do not defile the Three Treasures*. "Living the Dharma with the whole body and mind is the heart of wisdom and compassion. Virtues return to the ocean of reality; just bow and serve." The best way to understand this precept is: to even give rise to the thought that there is a distinction between Buddhas and ordinary beings defiles the Three Treasures and violates this precept.

The Sixteen Precepts are not fixed rules of action or a code for moral behavior. They allow for changes in circumstances: for adjusting to the time, the particular place, your position, and the degree of action necessary in any given situation. What is appropriate at one time may not be appropriate at another. Times change, and it is imperative that we respond sensitively to the changes. The same is true regarding place. To wear my abbot's robe at the Monastery is appropriate; to wear it to the local diner is not. There is nothing wrong with the robe, but the meaning of its use changes from place to place. One's position in the context of a situation also influences action. What I do as a teacher, as a parent, or as a lover varies significantly. What is right in one role would be way out of line in another. For each of us our relative position has to be considered. Being sensitive to the degree of action necessary is also important. How much action is called for? Sometimes a whisper is sufficient; at another time a shout may be best. When we don't hold on to some idea of ourselves and a particular way we have to react, then we are free to respond openly, with reverence and consideration for all the life involved.

When we first begin practice, we use the Precepts as a guide for living our life as a Buddha. We want to know how to live in harmony with all beings, and we do not want to put it off until after we get enlightened. So, we practice the Precepts. We practice them the same way we practice the breath, or the way we practice a koan. To practice means to *do*. We *do* the Precepts. Once we are aware of the Precepts, we become sensitive to the moments when we break them. When you break a Precept, you acknowledge that, take responsibility for it, and come back to the Precept again. It's just like when you work with the breath in zazen. You sit down on your cushion and you vow to work with the breath, to *be* the breath. Within three breaths you find yourself thinking about something else, not being the breath at all. When that happens, you acknowledge it, take responsibility for it, let the thought go, and return to the breath. That is how you *practice* the breath, and that is how you practice the Precepts. That is how you practice your life. Practice is not a process for getting someplace; it is not a process that gets us to enlightenment. Practice is, in itself, enlightenment.

In the ceremony of Jukai, the student receives the Sixteen Precepts one at a time, and publicly vows to maintain them. A second aspect of the process of Jukai is the establishment of a deep bond with the teacher and with the particular lineage. The student receives a lineage chart that is drawn in a very interesting way. At the top of the chart, the *Dharmakaya*, or ground of being, is depicted as a circle. Out of that pure Dharmakaya, a line is drawn to the first name in the chart, Shakyamuni Buddha. The line then continues to Mahakashyapa, and from Mahakashyapa to Ananda, and so on through the successive generations in India, China, Japan, and finally to this country and this teacher. The last name on the chart is that of the person receiving the Precepts. Then the line returns back into the original Dharmakaya circle, closing the loop, and forming a gigantic circle that is none other than the pure Dharmakaya itself. When you receive the Precepts you place yourself in that great circle. You are saying that your life and the life of all Buddhas past, present, and future are the same life.

The new Buddhist also receives a Dharma name during the Jukai ceremony. Receiving a new name is common to many rites of passage and most religions. In Zen the new name becomes a kind of koan for the student. It is selected very carefully by the teacher to reflect the student's personality and to help guide their practice. A name tends to function like an access word, just as a key symbol might be used to access a certain program in a computer. We may change our name as we get older, so Annie might become Ann—a little more dignified. But when someone calls, "Annie," or "Junior," a button is pushed, a program opens up, and suddenly our six- or seven-year-old self begins to respond. When we receive a Dharma name, suddenly we have a clean slate. The name has no history except the history that we now begin to create with it. It may take a while to get used to a new name, to know how to respond to it. Gradually, you find that people identify you with that name, and your practice begins to reflect it.

During the ceremony new Buddhists also receive a *rakusu*, or miniature *kesa*, representing the robe of the Buddha. During the training week, each recipient has sewn his or her own rakusu, chanting with each stitch, "Being one with the Buddha, being one with the Dharma, being one with the Sangha." As you might imagine, by the end of that week, a tremendous amount of energy is contained in that rakusu. It forever serves as a reminder to the student of what their life is about. Each morning in the zendo, we place our kesa on our head and chant, "Vast is the robe of liberation, a formless field of benefaction. I wear the Tathagatha's teaching, saving all sentient beings." This is the vow of the bodhisattva to work for all sentient beings; it functions as a way to not forget what our practice is, what the Precepts are, what the vows are that we have made.

It is one thing to receive the Precepts, but the real point of practice is to *be* the Precepts through and through, to manifest them with our lives. When you *are* the Precepts, you realize that there is no giver and no receiver, and that there is nothing to give and nothing to receive.

The Precepts are a sword that kills and a sword that gives life. The sword that kills is the absolute basis of reality, no-self. The sword that gives life is the compassion that comes out of that realization of no-self. The Precepts are the sword of the realized mind. The time to receive them is when they are already manifest in your life.

The Precepts need to be understood clearly from the literal point of view, from the perspective of compassion and reverence for life, and from the absolute, or "one-mind," point of view. Their richness is wasted if we see them simplistically as a set of rules, a list of "dos and don'ts." They are not meant to bind but to liberate. In fact, they define a life that is unhindered, complete, free. What the Precepts do is to bring into consciousness that which is already there. What the ceremony does is to bring the commitment being made into awareness, not only for oneself but for the entire sangha.

Precepts training obviously encompasses much more than the special week preceding Jukai; in a sense, it is part of just about everything that happens at the Monastery. Throughout the year, the Precepts are taken up in mondo or Dharma Combat as dialogues on ethical and moral points, in workshops on ethics and morality; and through *Fusatsu*, the ceremonial renewal of vows.

When one only reads about Buddhism, one can come to the conclusion that Zen is amoral, that it considers itself above morality and does not address itself to ethical teachings. That is the view of a person standing on the sidelines, only involved intellectually. Those who truly embrace this practice cannot help but see the intimacy between the Buddhadharma and a moral and ethical life. It is intrinsic to the teaching itself. The life of the Buddha is the manifestation of compassion, but if you do not engage it, it does nothing. It all depends on you. To stand on the sidelines merely thinking about practice is *Buji Zen*. For the teachings to come alive, they have to be lived with the whole body and mind.

I feel that because we put such an emphasis on the Precepts, we have a moral obligation to do something about that misconception concerning Zen and morality. There are thousands of Zen practitioners in our country, many thousands who have received the Precepts and taken refuge in the Three Treasures but who don't really know what they've done. They have no idea what the Precepts mean. Try asking someone when you see the little red cord around their neck what it really means to take refuge in the Three Treasures. Ask yourself what it means to take refuge in the Three Treasures. What is refuge? What, really, are the Three Treasures? We say "Buddha, Dharma, and Sangha," but what does that mean? Those are the words. What is the reality of Buddha, of being one with the Buddha, being one with the Dharma, being one with the Sangha? It is not some idea. It is a reality, a state of consciousness, a state of being. It is the state of being in harmony with the moral and ethical teachings.

We live in a time period of considerable moral crisis, with an erosion of values and a fragmentation of meaning prevalent throughout the fabric of the society. The crisis impacts on us personally, as a nation, and as a planet. The injuries that we inflict on each other and on our environment can only be healed by sound moral and ethical commitment. That doesn't mean being puritanical. It doesn't mean being "moralistic." These Precepts have a vitality that is unique in the great religions of the world. They are alive, not fixed. They function broadly and deeply, taking into account the intricacies and subtleties of conditions encountered through intimate identification.

There is so much to learn. The Precepts are incredibly profound. Don't take them lightly. They are direct and confrontive, and they are subtle. Please use them. Press up against them. Push them. See where they take you. As you explore their edges in your own encounters, and discover problems, bring those problems to dokusan as a koan. I'll be happy to teach you.

Whether you have taken the Precepts or not, whether or not you even intend to, you are free to use them. When you have been using them, when you feel they are part of your life and are at ease with working with them, then the Precepts have been transmitted and received. That is the time to do the ceremony. So, please take them. Make them your own. They are no small thing, by any measure. They nourish, they heal, and they give life to the Buddha.

6. PAINTING SPRING:
ART PRACTICE

Master Dogen, addressing the assembly, said:

My late master, old Buddha (T'ien-t'ung Ju-ching), said, "The original face has no birth and no death, Spring is in the plum blossoms and enters into a painting." When you paint Spring, do not paint willows, plums, peaches, or apricots, but just paint Spring. To paint willows, plums, peaches, or apricots is to paint willows, plums, peaches, or apricots — it is not yet painting Spring. It is not that Spring cannot be painted, but aside from my late master, old Buddha, there is no one in India or China who has painted Spring. He alone was the sharp, pointed brush who painted Spring. This Spring is Spring in the painting because it enters into a painting. He does not use any other power, but lets plum blossoms activate Spring. He lets Spring enter into a painting and into a tree — this is his skillful means. Because my late master, old Buddha, clarified the *Treasury of the True Dharma Eye,* he correctly transmitted it to the Buddhas and ancestors who assembled in the ten directions of past, future, and present. In this way, he thoroughly mastered the eyeball and opened up the plum blossoms.

This was written on the sixth day, eleventh month, first year of Kongen, 1243, at Yoshimi Monastery, Yoshita County, Echizen Province. Deep snow, three feet, all over the earth.

Master Dogen is one of the spiritual giants of history and one of the greatest religious teachers of Japan. He was an incredible poet, mystic, and philosopher, compiling many of his major works while in his thirties. This translation of "Plum Blossoms" is another of the sections of his master work, *Shobogenzo: Treasury of the True Dharma Eye.*

"When you paint Spring do not paint willows, plums, peaches, or apricots, but just paint Spring." What is Dogen talking about when he says, "just paint Spring?" What is Spring? He says that "Spring is in the plum branch covered with snow." In that withered-looking single branch sticking out from under the snow at thirty-below-zero, there is Spring. Why can't we see it? Why can't it be seen? "Even though the attainment of realization is immediately manifest, its intimate nature is not necessarily realized. Some may realize it and some may not." Just paint Spring.

Master Dogen writes in another fascicle, "The Way of Everyday Life," that "Seeing forms with the whole body and mind, hearing sounds with the whole body and mind, one understands them intimately." By definition, "intimately" means that there is no separation. To "be intimate" means to be the thing itself. Ti-ts'ang once asked Fa-yen, "Joza, where have you come from?" "I pilgrimage aimlessly," replied Fa-yen. "What is the matter of your pilgrimage?" asked Ti-ts'ang. "I don't know," replied Fa-yen. "Not knowing is most intimate," remarked Ti-ts'ang. At that, Fa-yen experienced great enlightenment.

In intimacy there is no internal dialogue letting you know that you are sitting well or not sitting well, constantly evaluating, comparing, analyzing, judging. The witness disappears — there is no body, no mind, no self, no other. No subject or even object of your attention exists. When you are the thing itself, it pervades the whole universe. When the thing itself pervades the whole universe, the reference system that we use to evaluate, analyze, judge, understand, and know is gone. How can you possibly know? A student says, "I was in deep samadhi." I ask, "What was it like?" She says, "Well, it was all black and then I felt this and then I felt that." In deep samadhi there is no way to evaluate; there is no sense of time or space. There is "no eye, ear, nose, tongue, body, mind; no color, sound, taste, touch, or phenomenon; no world of sight, or consciousness" What are you going to evaluate with? That is the intimacy that Master Dogen is speaking of. That is the intimacy of "when you walk, just walk; when you cry, just cry; when you laugh, just laugh."

One of the Kamakura-period koans is similar, on the surface, to what is going on here. Artists and samurai warriors flocked by the thousands to the monasteries to learn Zen during the Kamakura period, the samurai because they were very concerned about being free from the question of life and death and had heard that Zen monks had it resolved, and the artists because they found that there was a particular kind of aesthetic in Zen that affected the way of perceiving painting, architecture, sculpture, and other arts. What we do here at Zen Mountain Monastery is very much a part of that Kamakura spirit, with the important distinction that we don't engage in what became in Japan a kind of "watered down" version of Zen in order to make it palatable to artists. We don't dilute it at all. It is the whole thing — you get it or you don't get it.

At that time, Zen literature and koans were written in classical Chinese, which very few Japanese could speak or read. Also, the study of these koans required a profound understanding of Chinese poetry. So, Kamakura masters redid the koans to make them more Japanese, more understandable.

One of these koans is called "Painting the Nature." It deals with Ichu, a famous painter and Zen teacher, the seventh master of Jifuku-ji. One day Nambutzu, a great warrior, came to see him and asked whether he could paint the fragrance described in a famous line of poetry: "After walking through the flowers, the horse's hoof is fragrant." Ichu drew a horse's hoof with a butterfly fluttering around it. Then Nambutzu quoted the line, "Spring breeze over the river bank," and asked for a picture of the breeze. Ichu drew a branch of waving willow. Nambutzu cited the famous Zen phrase, "A finger directly pointing to the human mind; see the nature to be Buddha," and asked for a picture of the mind. Ichu picked up the brush and flicked a spot of ink onto Nambutzu's face. The warrior was surprised and annoyed; Ichu rapidly sketched the angry face. Nambutzu then asked for a picture of "the nature." Ichu broke the brush. Nambutzu didn't understand, and Ichu remarked, "If you haven't got the seeing eye, you can't see it." Nambutzu asked him to take another brush and paint a picture of the nature. Ichu replied, "Show me your nature and I'll paint it." Nambutzu had no words. There are test questions for this koan, including: How do you show the Nature? Come, see your nature and bring proof of it! Say something on behalf of Nambutzu!

In this koan, needless to say, the questions and the way the master responded to them are at a very different level of understanding than what Dogen refers to when he speaks of his teacher, T'ien-t'ung Ju-ching. "It is not that Spring cannot be painted, but aside from our late master, Old Buddha, there is no one in India or China who has painted Spring. He alone was the sharp, pointed brush who painted Spring." Painter, brush, canvas, image, subject — they are not many. The painter *is* the brush, the image *is* the painter, the subject *is* the object, the canvas *is* the paint. Those things only separate themselves when we separate them by the way we use our mind. Whether you are speaking of a painting, Mu, a tree, a Buddha, or a plum branch — how you see it, how you relate to it has to do with how you live your life, with the question of life and death itself. "To paint willows, plums, peaches, or apricots is to paint willows, plums, peaches, or apricots;

it is not yet painting Spring." How do you paint Spring? "This Spring is the Spring in the painting because it enters into a painting. He does not use any other power, but lets plum blossoms activate Spring. He lets Spring enter into a painting and into a tree, this is the skillful means." How do you manifest the sharp, pointed brush that paints Spring?

"To forget the self is to be enlightened by the ten thousand dharmas. To be enlightened by the ten thousand dharmas is to cast off body and mind of self and other." The ten thousand dharmas are the whole phenomenal world. To be enlightened by the whole phenomenal world is to cast off body and mind of self and other. To be enlightened by the painting of Spring is to enter into Spring itself. Spring enlightens the painter, the painter enlightens Spring. Self is forgotten, Spring is forgotten. He "lets the plum blossoms activate Spring" — no other power is used.

"Because my late master, Old Buddha, clarified the *Treasury of the True Dharma Eye,* he correctly transmitted it to Buddhas and ancestors who assembled in the ten directions of past, future, and present. In this way, he thoroughly mastered the eyeball and opened up the plum blossom." The "eyeball" referred to here is the Dharma eye, the Buddha's eye. But how is it that his old master T'ien-t'ung Ju-ching thoroughly and correctly transmitted this "True Dharma Eye" to Buddhas and ancestors — including the ones who preceded him, the ones who were in his presence, and the ones who followed him? He transmitted into the past, present, and future. Kasho Buddha, one of the legendary past seven Buddhas, died long before the Buddha was born. How is it that he transmitted to him? How is it that the act of realization penetrates both forward and backward?

Every act of karma does that. We think of karma as affecting only the future, but it also affects the past and the present. If you want to understand the past, look at the present. If you want to know the future, look at the present. This very moment is past, present, and future. Mount Gridhrakuta is here on this mountain. *The Treasury of the True Dharma Eye* of this very moment walks forward and backward in time.

"He correctly transmitted it to the Buddhas and ancestors who assembled in the ten directions of past, future, and present. In this way he thoroughly mastered the eyeball and opened the plum blossom." What is the opening of the plum blossom? It is to be enlightened by the ten thousand dharmas, by the whole phenomenal universe. To be enlightened by the whole phenomenal universe is to forget the self, and to forget the self is to "cast off body and mind of self and other." Then, "no trace of enlightenment remains and this traceless enlightenment continues endlessly."

"This was written on the sixth day, eleventh month, first year of Kongen at Yoshimi Monastery, Yoshita County, Echizen Province. Deep snow, three feet, all over the earth." "All over the earth" is right here now! The snowflake falls no place but here. No place but here is all over the earth — all over the universe. "Fields and mountains all taken by the snow… Nothing remains."

"If doubt arises and you think that plum blossoms are not Gautama's eyeballs, you should consider whether anything other than plum blossoms should be seen as eyeballs. If you seek the eyeballs elsewhere, you will not recognize them even though you are facing them because the meaning is not consummated. This day is not this day of an individual, but it is this day of the great house. Right now you should realize the plum blossoms as eyeballs. Stop seeking any further." What does he mean, to realize the plum blossoms as eyeballs? Another translation of this passage reads: "If we're deluded and think that the plum blossom is not the enlightened eye…" Notice that what one translation expresses as "eyeball" another calls "the enlightened eye." The translation continues, "It is not the enlightened eye of Shakyamuni. We should ask ourselves if there is any other vision besides this. You should know that if you seek enlightenment outside of plum blossoms you will not get it even if it is right in your hands. Even if it is in front of your face, you will not see it. Today is not our day, but the day of the Buddha Way. Right now we must open up the enlightened eye of the plum blossoms and stop chasing after other things." The plum blossom — what is it? What is the opening of the plum blossom? What is Gautama's eyeball, the eye of the Buddha? How will you "just" paint Spring?

People often say that the Soto School of Zen doesn't do koans, that it is the Rinzai School that uses koans. This is the master work of Dogen, founder of the Soto school in Japan, and just one of ninety-two chapters of the *Shobogenzo: The Treasury of the True Dharma Eye*. We're dealing with only three paragraphs of that chapter. In those three paragraphs are the following koans: What does it mean to just paint Spring? What is the sharp, pointed brush that paints Spring? How does Spring enter a painting? How does it enter the tree? How does he transmit to Buddhas of past, present, and future? What is it to master the eyeball and open the plum blossom? What is "deep snow, three feet, all over the earth"? What is the original face that has no birth or death? How does Spring in a plum blossom enter into a painting? These are all koans, and, needless to say, explanations won't reach them. In face-to-face teaching, the thing itself needs to be presented. Live words, not dead words — turning words that reveal "body and mind have fallen away."

"Fallen away body and mind" is not a zombie or corpse walking around, eyes rolled back, tongue pressed up against the upper palate, spaced out. It is alive, working, functioning, living, laughing, crying, dancing Zen, this-very-life-Zen, the only kind of Zen there is. Zen is not an activity that takes place in the world; Zen is the activity of the world itself. To paint Spring, to paint the eyeball of the Buddha, is to manifest *The Treasury of the True Dharma Eye*. To transmit to the Buddhas of past, present, and future is the life of each one us that is to be realized. T'ien-t'ung Ju-ching, the old Buddha said:

> *Bright and bright, clear and clear*
> *Do not seek only within the shadow of plum blossoms.*
> *Rain is created and clouds are formed*
> *throughout past and present*
> *Past and present, solitary and silent*
> *Where does it end?*

Clouds and rain are liberated from plum blossoms; past, present, and future are plum blossoms. Spring is activated from the power of plum blossoms. Where do you find yourself?

7. MIRACLE OF ALIVENESS:
BODY PRACTICE

Body practice is not exercise. It is not martial arts or aerobics, jogging or pumping iron. Body practice is nothing other than washing the face and cleaning the body; it is urination and elimination; it is cooking food and eating a meal; it is healing sickness, actualizing birth, practicing life, realizing death. Only when this is understood can we begin to speak of martial arts, aerobics, and pumping iron. Body practice is concerned with self-realization through the body. It is realizing that this body is the body of the Buddha, the body of this entire universe.

Self-realization needs to be with our whole being. Unfortunately, the search for self-knowledge is usually regarded as purely a function of the intellect. Feeling and intuition are largely considered to be subjective, and therefore unreliable, instruments for realizing truth. Yet by reducing the search for truth to an intellectual activity, we achieve only a distorted understanding of who we really are.

This has resulted in a view of religion, psychology, medicine, and politics in which the human condition is divided into discrete physical, mental, and spiritual parts. From this perspective, we tend to see the human body as the exclusive province of medicine, relegating the spirit to the world of religion, and the mind to that of psychology. Human emotion is left out entirely. Because of this compartmentalizing, we have a psychology that, in attempting to understand the mind, isolates it from the body. Medicine, on the other hand, in trying to heal the body, often ignores the mind. And, generally, in our religions the body is essentially denied, so that what religion generally calls morality is, in fact, an attempt to control the body. Naturally, this causes great conflict.

In the political realm, heads of state routinely separate so-called "political issues" from human experience. They quietly sit down to discuss megatons of destructive power, kill-quotas, and "acceptable" losses as if they were dealing with abstractions. Meanwhile, the flesh and blood creatures who are the subject of those discussions know that pain, suffering, and death are not abstractions and that there are no "acceptable" losses of human life from nuclear weapons. But until we yell loud enough, "It's not an abstraction! It's my life you're talking about, Mr. Politician, Mr. Negotiator!" politicians will continue making abstract, intellectual decisions that adversely affect the physical universe we share.

Luckily, some eyes are opening and we are beginning to discover the truth of the Buddhadharma realized 2,500 years ago, the truth that is the interrelationship and interpenetration of all things, the unity of body, mind, and spirit, the holographic nature of the universe wherein you cannot affect one part without affecting the totality.

Master Dogen wrote:

> You should see the truth that all the Buddhas of past, present, and future are awakened and practice the Way. They don't leave out their bodies and minds. To doubt this is already to slander them. As we reflect quietly on this matter it seems quite reasonable that our bodies and minds enact the Way and our desire for enlightenment is awakened truly with the Buddhas of the three periods past, present, and future.

The human body is not a hindrance to the realization of enlightenment; rather, it is the vehicle through which enlightenment is realized. In spite of, or perhaps because of, the very concreteness of the body and all of its peculiarities, we raise the bodhi mind. Through it we practice, realize enlightenment, actualize, and attain the Way. Because the body fills the mind and the mind penetrates the body, we call this "the permeation of body and mind." That is to say, body/mind is the entire universe in all of its directions.

Alfred North Whitehead once pointed out that when we really understand the biological and physiological functioning of the human body and the behavior of the molecules which constitute it, it becomes impossible to entertain the notion of a discontinuity between the body and its external environment. Living on this mountain, I can't help but realize that my body is completely integrated with the body of the mountain. Every time I drink the water that spills out of it into the mountain stream, the cells of my body assimilate it. My body is now largely composed of the water that comes from this mountain. We grow our food in the mountain's soil. The plants start out as a single seed and, by taking water, light, and minerals from the mountain, eventually manifest themselves as fruits, vegetables, flowers. Thus, we take the mountain into our very being; we consume it. Our septic system even returns our waste to the mountain. How could we feel separate from it?

A recent Fall Almanac carried an interesting article written by someone who must have had a great deal of time on his hands. This person was able to show what percentage of each lungful of the air we breathe today contains the same molecules of oxygen breathed by the Buddha, Napoleon, Aristotle, and even the dinosaurs. His calculations demonstrated constant recycling. The oxygen we take in to combust our lives produces carbon dioxide, which goes back into the atmosphere and is assimilated by plants, which then utilize and release it back to us as oxygen to breathe. This cycle of assimilating and returning the same atoms and molecules to the planet continues and has continued from generation to generation. To see ourselves as separate from the earth and from this universe is, at the very least, scientifically erroneous.

Master Dogen wrote:

> Although the body and mind are undefiled, there is the truth of cleansing the body and there is the truth of cleansing the mind. Not only does it purify the body and mind, but it purifies even the land and the trees. Lands have never been covered with dust and dirt, yet it is the desires of Buddhas to cleanse them. Attaining the fruit of Enlightenment they still do not retreat or abandon. Such a supreme principle is difficult to comprehend. Ritual conduct is the supreme principle. The realization of the Way is ritual conduct.

One of the important parts of training as laid down by Master Dogen is what he calls "purification." This purification gets down to the nitty-gritty of life itself. His teaching is that the daily actions of our life are sacred — they are the stuff of real liturgy. The "dust and dirt" he refers to are used as synonyms for defilement and ignorance. It is in this sense that "purification" is used in many Zen Buddhist ceremonies — including the birthing ceremony, Jukai (lay ordination as a Buddhist), and Tokudo (monk's ordination). It is not an attempt to be rid of pollutants, sins, or guilt, but rather the self-affirmation of original purity or emptiness, totally untouched by dualism. It involves neither the removal of impurity nor the seeking for purity. It is the simple act of using the bathroom, washing the face, brushing the teeth. Whether you are eating, working, or bowing, be present with the whole body and mind. Tune into yourself, into your body, into your life. Every act is not only a ritual in Zen — it is a sacrament.

Oryoki, the ritual meal, in making eating a conscious act, becomes a sacrament. Dogen quotes from the *Vimalakirti Sutra*:

> When a person is enlightened in their eating, all things are enlightened as well. If all Dharmas are non-dual,

humans are also non-dual in their eating. Indeed, Dharma is identified with one's eating and one's eating is identified with Dharma. For this reason, if Dharma is the Dharma nature, a meal is also the Dharma nature. If Dharma is thusness, food is likewise thusness. If Dharma is one mind, a meal is also one mind. If Dharma is enlightenment, food is enlightenment. Therefore, the act of eating constitutes the truth of all dharmas. This can be fully comprehended only among Buddhas. At the very moment we eat, we are possessed of ultimate reality: essence, substance, energy, activity, causation. So Dharma is eating, and eating is Dharma. This Dharma is enjoyed by Buddhas of past and future. This eating is full of holy joy and ecstasy.

According to Dogen, there are three types of "pure food": that which comes from trees and plants, that obtained from begging, and that donated by supporters. Anything that is given is purified by the act of giving, provided it is pure giving, done with an open heart, with no strings attached. And so it is with all things. The purity of the thing is determined by its origins, how we come by it. In complete *dana* (giving), there is no separation between the giver and the receiver. Similarly, because a *kesa* (monk's robe) is traditionally made of discarded rags and vile cloth that has been chewed by rodents, it is said to be made of "pure cloth." Golden, purple, or silken kesas should not be worn unless received as a gift.

The *tenzo* (chief cook) in a traditional Japanese Zen monastery is second only to the abbot, according to Dogen. The chief cook's job is first and foremost to nurture the monks and to ensure their well-being and peace. Dogen calls this an act of "nourishing the seeds of the Buddha." The cook is fully responsible for the monks' nourishment, not just physically, but morally and spiritually as well. He's not just a dietitian in the modern sense, but more like a religious teacher. Therefore, the chief cook's job is usually given to a very mature, older monk.

Dogen uses the example of Hsueh-feng as tenzo at Te-shan's monastery: "One day Hsueh-feng was washing the rice. Te-shan said to him, 'Do you wash the sand away from the rice or the rice away from the sand?'" This is a teaching about duality — about absolute and relative, good and bad, heaven and earth, man and woman. Dogen constantly addresses these dualities in terms of everyday affairs: rice and sand, purity and impurity. "Hsueh-feng said, 'I wash both rice and sand away at the same time.' [Hsueh-feng shows a side of it.] 'Then what will the Assembly eat?' [Te-shan brings up the other side.] Hsueh-feng covered the rice washing bowl with his body. Te-shan said, 'Someday, you will be a great teacher,' and left."

One ancient teacher said, "For a tenzo, working with his sleeves tied back is the activity of the Way-seeking mind." A tenzo has to be able to pick up a cabbage leaf and manifest it as the sixteen-foot golden body of the Buddha. The sixteen-foot golden body of the Buddha does not fall into the dichotomies of purity and impurity. In Christianity, people are considered tainted from the outset by "original sin," making them imperfect and susceptible to evil. Human life is one long struggle against this imperfect nature. Buddhism begins with original purity — with each one of us, just as we are, considered perfect and complete, lacking nothing. "Each abiding in its own Dharma state completely fulfills its virtues," Dogen writes. That means that each one of us, abiding in our Dharma state, completely fulfills our potential and capabilities. "No creature ever fails to cover the ground on which it stands."

Mind is body, body is mind. That is why working with the breath is so important in zazen. If the mind is agitated, the breath is agitated. When the mind is at rest, the breath is deep and easy, without hindrance or blockage. One of the precepts, in particular, points quite clearly to this body/mind continuity: the precept of "not clouding the mind." This refers to the need to abstain from drugs, alcohol, or any substance that would "defile our inherent purity." Drugs certainly have had a role to play in the Buddhadharma in America. In the fifties and sixties, for the most part, the people who were experimenting with drugs were the ones filing into the zendos.

After a number of years, the novelty of sitting wore thin and, gradually only more serious practitioners remained involved. But again and again, the question of drugs pops up and people come to teachers to test whether they have had an enlightenment experience when all they have had is a drug experience. It is just not the same thing. They are at opposite ends of the spectrum. Drugs either dull the mind or excite it tremendously. Using them to reach samadhi is about as effective as taking a baseball bat and hitting oneself on the head. It is important to recognize that for the falling away of body and mind, for the realizing of the self, alcohol and drugs are hindrances.

This is all part of the teaching of realizing with the body. Body practice means tuning into your body, into yourself. Not what you read, not what you're told, not what you think, but what you feel, what you experience with the body. Then you know what to eat, when to eat, how much to eat; how much to sleep, to run, to dance, to cry. That is being tuned into yourself. But that tuned-in feeling can also be deceptive, because one of the things we do is tune into feeling good. When you look carefully at addiction, it has to do with feeling good: drug addiction, alcohol addiction, nicotine addiction, sugar addiction, caffeine addiction. A good feeling is associated with the substance of addiction. And then there is the other side: the after-effect of the addiction. The drug wears off and there is pain; the alcohol wears off and there is a hangover; the cigarette wears off and there is a cough.

Besides having various effects on the user, these addictions also affect others. As we become aware of the addiction, we may choose to do something about it or we may, in fact, be unable to do anything about it. With respect to myself, I'm not very worried about my addiction to cigarettes because I'm not that worried about dying. But it does get to me when my son says, "Dad, please stop smoking," or when a student says to me, "Zen teachers get old, too. That cough sounds like it will be emphysema five years from now; that means another five years of decline and then you're dead. Our sesshins will dwindle from twelve a year to none. How will that help us?" That does affect me, as it affects them.

Taking responsibility for our life includes taking responsibility for our body. When sickness does come it is important to take responsibility for it. Master Yun-men, in teaching his community, said, "Medicine and sickness heal each other. The whole world is medicine. Where do you find the self?" When we are sick we'll usually pay the doctor to cure us, or say a prayer to God hoping that God will cure us. But this is not enough. Our health can't be left to someone else. We have to take that responsibility.

Dogen said, "Seeing forms with the whole body and mind, hearing sounds with the whole body and mind, one understands them intimately. Yet it is not like a mirror with reflections, nor like water under the moon — when one side is realized, the other side is dark." The human body and mind are united with the universe physically, psychologically, and spiritually. We are the body and mind of the Dharma, the Buddhas and ancestors, of the Tathagatha, the Way, the Three Realms, of heaven and earth, of the entire universe. Our body and mind are no other than the body and mind of the Buddha Way, the grasses, trees, mountains, rivers, wind, rain, water, and fire.

What, then, is body practice? It is not a matter of pumping iron or running a marathon. Body practice means realizing the Way with the body as well as with the mind. Just as in Chinese there is only one word for both "heart" and "mind" — *shin* — in Dogen's teaching there is no real distinction made between the words "body" and "mind." They function as one word. To study the Buddha Way is to study the self. To study the self is to be intimate with the self. The "self" means the whole body and mind. To be intimate with the self is to realize the ten thousand dharmas. There is nothing but the self. This is what our practice is. When we say "body and mind fallen away," that means to be intimate with the self. When we say to "forget the self," that means to be intimate with the self. When we say, to "cast off body and mind of self and other," that is nothing more nor less than being completely intimate with the self.

This, then, is the miracle of aliveness. This very life is the life of purity and perfection — lacking nothing. This very body is the body of the Tathagatha.

8. SACRED ACTIVITY: WORK PRACTICE

Our ordinary daily tasks can become wonderful opportunities to practice. When students reach a certain point of maturity in zazen, their work, their life, basically everything that they do, all develop an equivalent clarity and integrity. Work emerges as an active function of zazen.

The training at Zen Mountain Monastery provides an excellent chance to examine our habits, our way of doing things. The selflessness taught and practiced in the monastic environment, though, often conflicts with the self-indulgence generally encouraged in our society. In the zendo, we bow to each other; in the subway, we push each other. In the monastery, we serve; in the world, we take. The monastery can begin to seem like a sanctuary. But when seen more clearly, it is like a furnace within which, through our training, we can forge a life of strength and self-confidence to meet the situations we face every day. Our practice is not about isolating ourselves on some mountaintop, dwelling in tranquility while rejecting the busy activity of the world, but, rather, it is about manifesting the Buddhadharma in everything we do, so that the secular is, indeed, the sacred. This is what we need to see in order for the practice of work to function as an aspect of our Zen training.

There are many ways to practice work. We can look at it as just "a job to be done," or as simply a way to pass the time, to prevent boredom or idleness. We can, however, also look at it as a sacred activity, as a manifestation of the miracle of being alive. What we practice in the zendo is the "heart of the matter," the core that needs to express itself in every action. Zazen is not just sitting cross-legged on a pillow; it is growing a garden, getting to work on time, getting the job done.

The foundation of work practice is mindfulness, a state of consciousness in which the body is relaxed, the senses are alert, and the mind is clear and focused on the task at hand. This attentiveness is direct experience. Mindfulness is not static; it moves with the events of our daily life. There are times when we need to totally put ourselves into the task at hand. This is "holding fast," single-pointedly concentrating. At other times, it is necessary to "let go," to release and move on. Our tendency is to stick, moving on to the next activity while carrying all the debris of the last one with us. Mindfulness develops the ability to flow, concentrate, and remain in the present.

Some people have the misconception that planning and scheduling are not what Zen Buddhists do. But planning is not necessarily or solely goal-oriented; it exists right now. Scheduling exists right now. Without a plan, our work tends to become very scattered, inefficient, and ineffective. At the other extreme, we can get caught up in goals, forgetting that the goal and the process that brings us to that goal are the same reality, just as "good" and "bad" are the same reality, and heads and tails are two sides of the same coin. Each step, each action that brings us closer to the goal, *is* the goal itself. One is not before and the other after; both action and goal exist simultaneously. When we fully realize this, then our preoccupation with the goal disappears and we can be fully aware of the present moment. Then each step is vivid, and can be experienced totally.

One of the important parts of work practice is preparation, when everything required for the job is placed in a state of readiness. The work, tools, and materials are laid out. A number of years ago I began a process of ritualizing

170 THE EIGHT GATES OF ZEN

my preparations to photograph by taking very deliberate steps in laying out my camera, film, light meter, and other equipment, putting it all together as part of getting ready to go out and photograph. I found that the process also put my mind in a state of readiness, of awareness.

The Zen Arts are highly developed forms of work practice. In teaching a Zen Art, theory is rarely dealt with. The art is taught and communicated by practice itself. For example, the *sumi-e* artist teaching his students often does not speak a word in his first meeting with them. The class sits and waits; the master enters, bows to his students, and then proceeds to his work space. There, he carefully lays out his equipment — the paper, the brushes, the ink tray, the ink stick — and begins to examine the tools to select the ones he will use. Then he adds a bit of water to the tray and begins rubbing the ink stick in the tray very slowly, producing the ink.

This process in itself is a meditation, with each breath corresponding to one stroke in mixing the ink. When the right consistency and tone have been produced, he sets the stick aside, selects a brush, and carefully examines the blank paper. He sits in the presence of the empty space on the paper, feels the space, realizes the space fully. Then he wets his brush with just the right amount of ink and in a single breath executes a *zenga* painting, a whole landscape. The entire process may take half an hour to forty-five minutes of preparation and clean-up time, but the actual production of the painting takes place in a single breath.

Some of these masters have come to Zen Mountain Monastery over the years and we have had the opportunity to see them work, to see that single-pointedness of mind and attention to detail being practiced. Quite clearly there are characteristics common to all these teachers. Whether we are speaking of an accomplished painter, a master of the bamboo flute, or a teacher of the martial arts, there is inevitably a kind of spontaneity, professionalism, and free-flowing action evident.

Work practice can also be a teacher if we regard it that way. The teachings are everywhere if we have the eyes to see it. The rocks and water of the Esopus River expound the Dharma daily, if we have the ears to hear it. The bringing of the palms together in gassho is a reminder of the teaching that all dualities are part of the same reality. The left and the right hand come together as one thing: no separation. When I bow to the salt, I acknowledge that the salt and I are one thing. When I bow to you, I acknowledge that you and I are the same thing. When I bow to the Buddha, I acknowledge that it is the Buddha bowing to the Buddha. And so it is with work.

After the work is laid out, the next step is doing it. The art of this step is to really "do what you are doing while you are doing it" — in other words, to be fully present. To experience the breath in zazen is to *be* the breath. To experience the work is no different.

When the work is finished, there is a sense of completion, just like there is a sense of completion when you have finished a painting, a photograph, a performance. It is time to let go, time to bow and acknowledge the teaching. It doesn't matter whether you are bowing to something animate or inanimate; in either case, you are bowing to yourself. There is nothing outside you, unless you put it outside yourself, and you can only do that by the way you use your mind. To really complete work practice requires cleaning up, putting the tools away, picking up the loose ends, "leaving no trace." This means the dishes are washed and put away, the counters are wiped, the sink is clean, the floor is swept and mopped, the garbage is emptied. No trace remains that someone has eaten. Everything looks natural and ordinary. This also means not being excessive about it: "no trace" means no trace.

The problems we face in work function as our *genjokoans*, the koans of our everyday life. They can be handled in the same manner as the koans we work with in zazen. How do you deal with problems that come up when you are sitting in the zendo? When you are sitting, staying with your breath, you hear a sound that reminds you of something and suddenly you are a thousand miles away. The breath has been forgotten while you become immersed in whatever scenario you are developing. When you notice that you are not involved with the breath any longer, but are wrapped up in a thought, you look at the thought, acknowledge it, let it go, and come back to the breath. You don't evaluate it, analyze it, love it, or hate it. If the thought pops up again, you go through the process again: look at it, acknowledge it, let it go, and return your attention to the breath. Each time you bring the attention back to where you want it, you reinforce your power of concentration. And if the thought continues to recur, you let it happen. Be it. If fear keeps coming up, be the fear. Allow it and give it free range. Be the thing itself; don't separate from it. Each time you separate from it, it gets bigger. The more you pull away from it, the more powerful it becomes. Let it roam and then, after it has exhausted itself and completed its cycle, let it go and return to the breath.

The same process takes place with work practice. Each time you become distracted, you acknowledge what is happening, let the thoughts go, and return your attention to your work. Sometimes in work practice, just like in zazen, we get "stuck." This is what interview is for. You can use interview as an opportunity to look at and work with the problem in a different way. It becomes a koan. And the koans that arise out of your own sitting or out of your work are often the most powerful koans. A problem is an opportunity to really put yourself into your practice.

It is easy to practice when everything is going smoothly, but to sit hard is to sit when sitting is difficult. It is also the place that is generally the most productive, because the things that are most difficult for us almost always have the most to teach us.

Another aspect to consider in work practice is silence. Silence doesn't mean not speaking when it is necessary — in answering the phone, in giving instructions — but just cutting down on the unnecessary chatter, the talk that is there just for the sake of talking. When it is necessary to speak in order to communicate, we should do so. We should practice communicating. When it is time to be silent, we should be able to do that, too. This means not only being outwardly silent, but also silencing the inner dialogue, stilling our habit of constantly talking to ourselves. Practicing silence and avoiding idle talk helps develop the clarity, receptiveness, and concentration necessary for good work practice.

This way of working is not spacey, preoccupied, or trancelike: it is very much alive, awake, and alert, filled with life's force. It is the mind of the Way itself. What is the mind of the Way? Chao-chou once asked Nan-ch'uan, "What is the Tao?" Nan-ch'uan answered, "Ordinary mind is the Tao." "Then should we direct ourselves toward it or not?" asked Chao-chou. "If you try to direct yourself toward it, you go away from it," answered Nan-ch'uan. Chao-chou continued, "If we do not try, how can we know that it is the Tao?" Nan-ch'uan replied, "The Tao does not belong to knowing or to not knowing. Knowing is illusion; not knowing is blank consciousness. If you really attain to the Tao of no doubt, it is like the great void, so vast and boundless. How, then, can there be right and wrong in the Tao?" Ordinary mind — the mind that sleeps when it is tired and eats when it is hungry. This is the Buddha mind, the mind of work practice.

Layman P'ang said, "Isn't it wonderful? Isn't it marvelous? I chop wood and carry water." We should see that this life itself and all of its activity is the perfect manifestation of the Buddhadharma. This very life is the life of the Buddha, and the secular activities of this life are the Dharma itself. But we should be aware that, as Master Dogen says, "To carry the self forward and realize the secular is delusion; that the secular advances and realizes the self is enlightenment." To "carry the self forward" means to separate yourself. That the "secular advances" means to be one with the object of your attention. The secular world itself becomes your life, and its inherent liberation is constantly manifested.

If you still do not believe it, consider your breath for a moment. Bring it in from the atmosphere that surrounds you, taste it, fill your body with it, enjoy it. Now, let it go, return it to the environment... Isn't it a miracle, this life of ours?

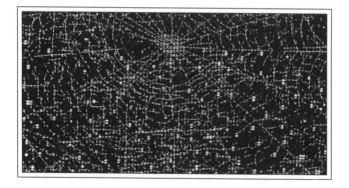

TWO PATHS

CLOUDS AND WATER

Zen Master Dogen said, "Those who regard secular life as an obstacle to the sacred know only that there is no sacredness in secular activities; they do not yet know that no secular activities exist in the sacred." In a way, we can see this as a gesture toward dissolving the differences between monk practice and lay practice. Yet, Dogen, and all of the masters in the history of Zen and of Buddhism, starting with the Buddha and coming down to present day teachers, have obviously favored monk practice since all of them were monks. Even the ones who became enlightened as lay practitioners usually received ordination before they transmitted the Buddhadharma to the next generation.

In creating the training matrix at Zen Mountain Monastery, one of the key things that we have done is to make a very clear separation between lay and monk practice. This is a new phenomenon on the landscape of the American Zen. Most of the lay practice that goes on in America is a slightly watered down version of monk practice, and most of the monk practice is a slightly glorified version of lay practice. In fact, there are controversies at most centers because frequently nobody can tell the difference between a monk and a lay person, except for the way they dress. Monks usually wear black robes and lay practitioners wear robes of another color. Most American monks live in the world, away from monasteries. They are householders who keep full-time jobs and have families. They don't shave their heads, and don't take vows that are different from the vows that lay practitioners take. This results in ambiguity and confusion. The hybrid path halfway between monk practice and lay practice reflects our cultural spirit of greediness and consumerism. With all the possibilities, why give up anything? I want it all. Why not do it all?

Within the Mountains and Rivers Order, there is a very clear distinction between monk and lay practice. In fact, we accent the differences, because the beauty of the relationship between the two practices depends upon those distinctions. You can't have co-origination and interdependence without differences. If everything were the same there would be no possibility of a relationship or realization.

The following prologue accompanies a koan dealing with the distinctions between monk and lay practice:

When sacred and secular are intermingled, even the great sages cannot distinguish between them. When monk and lay practice are interwoven, the fragrance of thousands of plum blossoms fill the ten directions. Even the Buddha fails to discern one from the other. To be unified with the Way is to be free and unhindered, whether in the mountain or in the marketplace, and in either to leave no trace of having entered.

Monk practice and lay practice are and always have been in a dynamic relationship, one supporting the other. You would have a very short-lived lay practice without monks and a very short-lived monk practice without lay practitioners. That has been the history of the Buddhadharma — 2,500 years of it — with its vitality and lifeblood depending on the contrast, the contact, and the integration of the two streams. This, of course, holds true for all dualities and it is the nature of the universe.

The Mountains and River Order distinguishes between monk and lay practice in several ways, but primarily with specific vows for monks, which are different from the lay practitioner's vows. Students who wish to enter monk practice first need to be Zen Mountain Monastery students, and then have to complete Jukai, which is the receiving of the Precepts. After a period of one year they can make the decision to enter the clerical track, or they can continue in the lay track. Those who stay in the lay track may become senior lay students, or shusos, when they reach the appropriate stage of training, trading in their beginner's gray robe for a white robe, symbolic of lay practitioners throughout the history of Buddhism, and particularly in Zen.

Students who decide at this stage to pursue the monk, or clerical, track, put on black robes instead, and after at least two years of postulancy and novitiate, may take monk's ordination. There are five monk's vows in addition to the Precepts: vows of stability, service, simplicity, selflessness, and to accomplish the Buddha's Way.

Note that the last vow does not say "accomplishing the Buddha Way," but "accomplishing the *Buddha's Way*," that is, to live the life that the Buddha lived. The Buddha Way is the teachings of the Buddha. All practitioners make the vow to accomplish the Buddha Way. The monk's vow is to accomplish the Buddha's Way, that is, to make real in one's own life the life of the Buddha, to actualize one's life the way historical Buddha did. To accomplish the Buddha's Way is not a place. It is not a goal. It doesn't have anything to do with time and space. It's a continuum. It's a continuum that goes back to the beginningless beginning. It's a continuum that proceeds into the far-distant future. It's a continuum that verifies the life of all Buddhas and is the realization of all Buddhas.

Why would a person choose such a path? This was a koan posed by Nagarjuna:

Nagarjuna said, "When lay trainees can become Bodhisattvas and enter nirvana, why is it necessary to take monk's ordination?" And then he answered himself, "The difference in path is not the objective, enlightenment, but the degree of difficulty in attaining this. It is most difficult for the lay person because of other responsibilities, much easier for the monks, who can fully devote themselves to practice."

A brahmin asked Shariputra, "What is the most difficult thing in the world?" Shariputra replied, "To renounce fame, fortune, property, and family and enter the Buddhist monkhood."

Dogen, although often speaking of lay practice and monk practice as being identical, elsewhere in his writings emphasizes the distinctions, making the same point as Nagarjuna. The enlightenment of a monk or a lay practitioner is not different. Both monk practice and lay practice can result in deep, profound realization; one indistinguishable from the other. What is different is the respective occupations of monks and lay practitioners, the difficulty of attaining realization, and the possibility of completing the training — what people do with realization before, during, and after it happens. From Nagarjuna's point of view, it's much easier to do monk's practice than it is to do lay practice.

In the world, we have many responsibilities and gravitate in many directions: family, job, property, children, neighborhood. As one develops as a lay practitioner, these activities and the thrust of one's life take place within the matrix of the Dharma, but the main focus of lay life remains one's family and career.

The focus of a monk's life is the Dharma matrix itself. A monk is married to the Dharma. The major occupation of a monk is the Dharma. Nothing else. One hundred percent of the time, every day. A monk has essentially one vow, and that vow is the Dharma. It's a vow of service, it's a vow of stability, it's a vow of selflessness, it's a vow of simplicity.

In traditional Zen writings, the term "monk" is not used; rather, there is the word *unsui*. Unsui literally translates as "clouds and water." Clouds and water are free. Clouds follow the wind, water the shape of the terrain. Nothing holds them back. If you try to stop a stream, it just builds up behind the obstruction and goes over it. The journey to the ocean is unstoppable. The biggest dam in creation can't hold back the river in its flow. It is persistent, continuous, flexible.

Yet, in a practical sense, one can ask: "What good is a monk?" Our society certainly posits that question, not just in relation to Zen monks, or Buddhist monks, but for monks in general. What does a monk produce? In a materialistic culture, where such incredible value is placed on productivity, what does a monk contribute? What good is such a life? What is the relevance of a monk to the world?

Thomas Merton once had something to say about this issue in his *Asian Journal*. He wrote:

> Are monks and hippies and poets relevant? No, we're deliberately irrelevant. We live with an ingrained irrelevance which is proper to every human being. The marginal person accepts the basic irrelevance of the human condition, an irrelevance which is manifested above all by the fact of death. The marginal person, the monk, the displaced person, the prisoner, all these people live in the presence of death, which calls into question the meaning of life. They struggle with the fact of death in themselves, trying to seek something deeper than death, because there is something deeper than death, and the office of the monk or the marginal person, the meditative person, is to go beyond death. Even in this life to go beyond. To go beyond the dichotomy of life and death and to therefore be a witness to life.

Is this, then, a life of total freedom? From one point of view, those who haven't renounced the world are caught up in the world, are holding on to the world, and are controlled by the world. They are not free to go from one place to another. They have responsibilities and obligations. At the same time, looking at it from the other side, a monk, following a strict monastic schedule and bound by monastic vows is completely in the hands of the teacher in a way that no lay practitioner could possibly be. If I wanted one of the monks to go to New Zealand and stay there, that is where they would go. If someone said, "You can't practice Zen Buddhism in New York State anymore," or if we lost the building and the grounds, and I had to move to California, the monks would follow me there. Why? Because there is nothing holding them back. They have no obligations other than to the Dharma.

Shukke-tokudo, monk's ordination, literally means "leaving home," giving up one's last name and taking on a monk's name. The bows that we do in gratitude to our parents during Jukai, are bows of good-bye for the home-leaver. "Thank you for this life." With monk's ordination, the relationship between the parent and the child completely changes. The child's obligation to care for the parents is replaced with a vow to serve all sentient beings, equally, without discrimination.

Leaving home doesn't mean ignoring one's family, however. That is one of the tremendous misconceptions about monk practice that persists in this country, one that I personally don't accept and don't practice. Yet, Zen literature does present examples that seem to imply that leaving home requires cutting family ties completely. Master Tung-shan, for example, after he left home, disregarded his mother when she got very old and came asking to be admitted to his monastery. She was clawing at the door, crying for help. She died, according to the story, of a broken heart. He wouldn't let her in. The story then continues, telling how she was reborn in some heaven and thanked her son for not breaking his vows as a monk. Well, I don't buy it. If one takes a vow to save all sentient beings, surely that includes one's own mother. Doesn't she deserve, at least, an equal opportunity with the rest of sentient beings?

At Zen Mountain Monastery monks can either practice celibacy or be in a stable relationship. But they have to make a vow not to procreate. If they do have a child, then they're a parent, not a monk. They have to take off their robes, raise the child until he or she is independent, and then they automatically, spontaneously, and miraculously become monks again. They put their robes back on and continue their monk practice. But as long as they've created another human being, they have a primary responsibility to that human being. Similarly, if someone has unfinished business with their family, they need to take care of that before taking monk's vows. They need to really leave home. This doesn't mean that monks ignore their parents or other family members. It just means that they have a relationship with them like with any other sentient being. If a person is in need, and they're the most appropriate one to give them nourishment and take care of them, it's fine for them to do it. I like to think of our practice as a very human practice.

Every fifth day the monks shave their heads and chant the *Gatha on Shaving the Head.* The gatha says, "In the drifting, wandering world, it is very difficult to cut off our human ties. Now, I cast them away and enter true activity. It is in this way that I express my gratitude. As I shave my head, I renew my vows to live a life of simplicity, service, stability, selflessness, and to accomplish the Buddha's Way. May I manifest my life with wisdom and compassion, and actualize the Tathagatha's true teaching."

How do these vows manifest themselves here in the twentieth century on Tremper Mountain? Taking a vow of poverty, the monks receive no salary and are not permitted to own any property. As a result, they become totally dependent upon the lay practitioners. If suddenly all the lay practitioners disappeared, the monks would have to go out and work in order to feed themselves. With the Monastery's main mortgage paid off, we don't have to worry about the rent anymore, but we still have to pay for the utilities. So, the food and the shelter are provided by the lay sangha practicing here. The monks offer their service to the community in a spirit of selflessness. This mutual dependency between the monks and the lay practitioners creates an essential part of the dynamic of these buildings and grounds, and of this Dharma. It allows for true giving to be practiced.

The vow of stability has to do with having completed the major changes in one's life. That is, no vows, above the vow to the Dharma, are functioning. There is a stable base, with all of the person's energy available to the Dharma. There are no other, superseding responsibilities or obligations. The monks with their commitment bring a sense of security for me. They are the continuation of this Dharma. Their vows assure that the Dharma of this mountain would go on, even after the buildings disappear and the mountain itself crumbles. No matter where, no matter how, it would continue. And it is for this reason that it has been so important to me, to my teacher, and to his teacher, who are all monks, to have completely dedicated monks among our successors.

If this sangha consisted solely of lay practitioners, it would be very lopsided. It would be very difficult, if not impossible, to operate a monastery. The central continuity that we have had from year to year, over the past twelve years, has been maintained by the monks. The changes, the comings and goings of the lay practitioners are quite dramatic. People come into residency for a year or two and then they leave. Others appear. There are a lot of unpredictability and fluctuations of interest. The stability rests with the monks. As we move into the future, that becomes more and more important. So, it is paramount to understand that the dynamic of monk practice/

lay practice, the interpenetration of sacred and secular, is a two-way street. You can't do it with one or the other alone.

It is just like the relationship of the absolute and the relative. As the *Sutra of the Identity of Relative and Absolute* says, absolute alone is not yet enlightenment. In fact, dwelling solely in the absolute is considered "making a living in a ghost cave," a dead end. It has no life, no vitality. Dwelling only in the relative, on the other hand, is complete delusion, being caught up in the words and ideas that describe reality, the world of this and that. But when you have both of them, and they interpenetrate freely, you have a dynamic relationship that creates "thousands of plum blossoms with their fragrance filling the ten directions." The plum blossom is an image for the Buddha. From beneath three feet of snow, a single plum branch extends. That's the Buddha's enlightenment. And from that branch, the blossoms, the fragrance, and the seeds of subsequent, endless generations appear.

When you have the two components, you have what it takes. The bee and the blossom are both necessary in order for the fruit to appear on the tree. If there's no cross-fertilization, you don't get any fruit. If there's no fruit, there's no ripening. If there's no ripening, there are no seeds. If there are no seeds, there are no succeeding generations. The interactive relationship is essential.

"When monk and lay practice are interwoven, the fragrance of thousands of plum blossoms fills the ten directions and even the Buddha fails to discern one from the other." To be unified with the Way is to be free and unhindered, whether in the mountain (mountain meaning the monastery) or in the market place (the market place being the world). And in either case, to be unified with the Way is to leave no trace of having entered.

So, we are back to Nagarjuna's question: "Why take monk's ordination?" There are hundreds of rationalizations

for becoming a monk. There are hundreds of rationalizations for being a lay practitioner. I remember the days I spent
debating these issues and justifications with my Dharma
brother, Tetsugen, and the other monks at Zen Center of Los
Angeles, while I was a lay practitioner, a proud-to-be lay
practitioner; white robed, bearded, long-haired, in the image of Layman P'ang and Vimalakirti. I saw monk practice
as a useless device, unnecessary in our century. And then,
somehow, something changed, and I saw it differently. It
wasn't a matter of one being better than the other. It was a
matter of clarifying that difference and seeing the unity of
that duality. If you go to the words and ideas to try to
understand this process, you're lost. "If you're responding
to devices and entering into forms, you're far from your true
home." It's got nothing to do with the surface characteristics
of these things. It's got nothing to do with hair or no hair;
black robe, white robe; in the world, in the monastery.
There's something else going on. What is it?

"A brahmin asked Shariputra, 'What is the most difficult thing in the world?' Shariputra replied, 'To renounce
fame, fortune, property, and family and enter the
Buddhist monkhood.'" From Shariputra's perspective, to
enter monkhood is the ultimate human endeavor. Yet,
monk practice in America, in general, does not currently
call for that degree of renunciation. There are Buddhist
lineages in Asia that do so to this day, but even in Japan
some of the wealthiest people I ever met were temple
priests. Priests' incomes were extraordinary, often in
excess of half-a-million dollars a year. The temples are
run like a family business. The priests are married
and have children. Sons frequently succeed their fathers
and become the next owners of the business, which frequently involves little more than doing Buddhist funerals.

At Zen Mountain Monastery, our intent is to return to
the tradition of whole-hearted monk practice. Much of

what we have been doing here is in accord with the classical Buddhism of the Chinese T'ang Dynasty, with a lot of consideration given to Western monastic models as well. Despite the comments of several Western writers and some Theravadin teachers that the West has no model for monastic practice, we found that the West has a long and distinguished history of monasticism.

We looked at and borrowed from that rich heritage born of Western tradition, and combined it with the classic Chinese forms, to create the foundation for this monastery. The Anglican monastics who live only a few miles from Zen Mountain Monastery have been a particularly valuable resource to us for creating a Western Zen Buddhist form of monasticism. That's where the models for our postulancy and novitiate program originated. The Asian traditions don't have that. The closest thing to it is the tradition of ordaining *shami* monks. Shami monks are traditionally ordained at a very young age, as early as eleven years. The date of their ordination establishes their seniority, which will become important later in their careers.

Our postulancy and novitiate program more closely resemble the ones that operate in Roman Catholicism and Anglican monasticism. They are periods of time when people have an opportunity to experience the monastic life directly, before officially embracing the vows. It is time of deep search while working closely with the teacher and clarifying one's relationship with the Dharma.

Our form of monasticism borrows significantly and, yet, differs significantly from both the Asian and the Western models. It's a unique system. A critical underlying attribute of it is its dynamic relationship with lay practice. Each nourishes the other. There have been very deeply enlightened lay practitioners throughout history. But, somehow, their lineages never continued for long. There hasn't been a lay lineage ever in the history of Zen that has lasted more than two or three generations. I don't know what the reason is, but that's been the limit. The only exception to that may be — and we'll see, only time will tell — the Yamada lineage that is now continuing into its third generation. That's about the longest that a lay lineage has maintained itself. It's extraordinary when you think about it. Two thousand five hundred years, all of these incredible lay practitioners that have appeared here and there, and somehow it didn't continue. Is it because of the lack of institution?

The footnotes to the koan clarify the following points.

The koan starts off with *Nagarjuna said...* and the footnote says, "Since time immemorial, it has been the way of the teachers of our school to create waves where there is no wind. If you want to know where he's coming from, it's not hard."

The next line says *When lay trainees can become Bodhisattvas and enter nirvana...* and the footnote, "He can't be called a petty thief. He has no shame, so he asks such a question. The Dharma is gateless; where is there an entry point?" He speaks of Bodhisattvas entering nirvana. What is the point of entry into nirvana?

The next line asks *Why is it necessary to take monk's ordination?* The footnote says, "He uses his power to mystify the people. Immeasurably great people inevitably bog down in words and ideas. Still, he wants people to understand." That's one of the reasons why teachers from time immemorial have created these complications, playing the role of the fool, asking stupid questions and giving stupid answers, just simply because they want people to understand. That's why he brings this up.

And so he answered himself. The footnote comments, "Devil's mask, god mask, seeing a cage he builds a cage." A cage is where people are stuck. A teacher's antidote for the cage is another cage. Medicine and sickness heal each other.

And then the next line: *The difference in the path is not in the objective, enlightenment,...* The footnote says, "If you direct yourself toward it, you move away from it" *...but in the degree of difficulty in attaining this.* "What's he saying? This old teacher is covered with mud. *It* can't be attained." Why does he speak of the difficulty in attaining it, when from the very beginning, it's unattainable? It can't be received, can't be given. What's he talking about?

It is most difficult for the lay person because of other responsibilities. Footnote says, "Not difficult, not easy. Like when the wind blows from the east, the leaves gather in the west." It's not a matter of difficult or easy.

The next line: *It's much easier for the monks, who can fully devote themselves to the practice.* And the footnote, "Not easy, not difficult. Like the endless river finding its way to the great ocean." In a sense, "difficult," "easy" is creating those dualities that fracture us at every turn. And it's no different with monk practice/lay practice, or monastery/world. We inevitably fall to one side or another. We leave the world of this and that and we come into practice in the Monastery, and then repeat the whole process all over again. Absolute and relative, good and evil, heaven and earth, sacred and secular. And it always comes down to: how do you transcend these dualities? I am not asking about your ideas or descriptions — what is the actual practical action?

That's what koan study is about, and it doesn't come from the movement of the mind followed by action. It's totally spontaneous. It arises of itself. People tend to get the idea that koan study is about answering questions, like it's some kind of an oral examination that takes place in the dokusan room. It has nothing to do with the words and ideas. To see a koan, the answer to a koan, is not a gesture, not a word, not a sentence. It's a state of consciousness. You can stand there on one leg with your thumb up your nostril — if your state of consciousness is right, you've seen the koan. If you've seen it, it reveals itself. If you haven't seen it, that too reveals itself. The only place these koans count is in this very life itself. So understanding is not enough; believing is not enough. Only realization itself transforms our lives. It's only in realizing that it manifests itself in the world. Words and ideas are wonderful for textbooks, but they aren't worth a damn when it comes to living our lives moment to moment to moment.

The next line: *A brahmin asks Shariputra...* The footnote says, "After all, if you don't ask, how will you ever know?" *What's the most difficult thing in the world?* "This seems like an odd quest. What will he do when he finds out?" Seems a little weird, doesn't it? You go around to a great master and say "What's the most difficult thing in the world?" Why do you want to know? That's what I would ask.

Shariputra replied, "To renounce fame, fortune, property, and family, and to enter the Buddhist monkhood." The footnote states, "As it turns out, he's too literal. At that moment, the brahmin should have given him a taste of Shariputra's own provisions." How would you, in place of the brahmin, give Shariputra a taste of his own provisions? What are his own provisions?

The koan concludes with a capping verse:
Householders and homeless living together.
Sacred and secular intermingled.
What kind of place is this?
Can't you see?
The diamonds in the great net reflect each other.

That great net of diamonds is the mythological Net of Indra, where every gem contains every other gem in the universe, past, present, and future. And each of those diamonds is each one of us. Their interpenetration is the fifth rank of Master Tung-shan, and it describes all of our relationships, all of the dualities. There's an entirely different, powerful, and dynamic way to perceive this universe that needs to be realized and actualized, in the mountain and in the market place.

The interdependence between monk practice and lay practice is the juice, the vital energy that will keep this Dharma alive on this continent for many generations to come. It's important that we as a sangha recognize it, that we nourish it and support its development. I would not want to see this sangha be all monks; I would not want to see it be all lay practitioners. We need both monk practice and lay practice, and both must be strong, each with an integrity and uniqueness of its own.

LOTUS IN THE FIRE

In coming from the East to the West, Buddhism has undergone a revolution in several different ways. The first of these is that Buddhism finds itself within cultures that guarantee freedom of religion as part of the law of the land. This is new, and it means that the Bodhisattva vow of compassion can be translated into social action without the danger of monks being beheaded and monasteries burned as a result. Buddhist groups here are very active in peace movements, ecology, and social welfare; in fact, some sanghas are totally dedicated to that kind of work.

The second area that is a significant manifestation of this revolution is the presence of women in the Dharma. In most of the training centers in the United States, close to forty percent of the practitioners are women. In our monastery, the ratio has even gone the other way: sixty percent women, forty percent men. Women teachers are beginning to emerge. That, in itself, is not unusual, as in the history of Buddhism there have always been women teachers. What is unusual is that so many have appeared. Many of the women teachers have men students, and that is quite new. There is a difference between men and women in their styles of teaching. All of this is sure to have an impact on the development of Buddhism over the next twenty to thirty years.

The third aspect of the current Buddhist revolution in the West is the visibility and strength of lay practice. Lay practitioners have always been a vital part of Mahayana Buddhism. The history of lay practice goes all the way back to the time of the Buddha and the great lay practitioner Vimalakirti. Vimalakirti was said to be as realized as the Buddha. Buddha himself recognized Vimalakirti as being an enlightened teacher. His teachings are compiled in the *Vimalakirti Sutra*, forming a particularly relevant text for lay practitioners. It is one of the five basic sutras that we study in Zen. It was during the times of Vimalakirti that the term "white-robed one" began to be used. White robes were worn by lay practitioners. With Vimalakirti, a precedent was set and the tradition of lay practice continued from that period on, throughout the history of Indian Buddhism, with many eminent lay teachers emerging.

It continued into China, where lay practice was exemplified by the P'ang family. Layman P'ang, his wife, and their daughter were all realized practitioners. *The Record of Layman P'ang* consists of their dialogues, impromptu conversations and Dharma combats that took place around the kitchen table and in the fields. Of the three, it is said that the daughter seems to have been by far the brightest and the clearest. Their lives are a history of lay practice.

Many of Chinese emperors and members of the official court were Buddhist practitioners. In China, the position of "National Teacher" was often held by a Zen master. Because he had the ear of the emperor, the National Teacher's role was quite powerful, with a direct ability to influence social action and government policies. Some of the greatest Buddhist masters in history were National Teachers, and most of their students were the lay practitioners of the time — members of the court, generals, emperors, and ordinary citizens.

Despite the continual presence of lay practice, however, the history of Mahayana Buddhism still remained dominated by monk practice and monasteries. It persisted that way throughout China, Korea, Vietnam, and Japan. Lay practitioners would inevitably appear at some monastery, study for a period of time with a respectable teacher, realize themselves, and leave. After being transmitted to, and becoming a master in their own right, a lay teacher would typically return to his or her community and teach there. What history shows us is that their lineages were short-lived. Their teaching continued only for a generation or two, and then faded out. Outside the traditional matrix of the monastery, transmission purely within lay practice had a difficult time maintaining itself.

Our own lineage, of which the Mountains and Rivers Order is a part, contains a branch that was transmitted through lay practitioners. My teacher, Maezumi Roshi, is a meeting point of three different Zen traditions. One lineage comes down through Master Dogen and the Soto school. The second branch is the Inzan Rinzai lineage, passed on through Yasutani Roshi. And the third tradition is the Takuju Rinzai lineage that was transmitted to Maezumi Roshi by Koryu Roshi. Koryu Roshi was a layman whose teacher asked him not to take the vows of a monk, but to continue his life as a lay practitioner. All of his successors were lay practitioners, with the exception of Maezumi Roshi who was already a monk when he received that lay transmission.

Another example of a classic lay lineage alive today is the branch of the Harada-Yasutani tradition practiced and taught by Aitken Roshi. Harada Roshi was a monk and Yasutani Roshi was a monk. Yasutani Roshi transmitted to Yamada Roshi who was a layman. Yamada Roshi was the director of a hospital; that was his main occupation. Upon transmission he began leading the Zazenkai, a sitting group that Yasutani Roshi had been teaching. Later, Yamada Roshi would transmit to Aitken Roshi, beginning a tradition of lay transmission. Aitken Roshi has now transmitted to the next generation.

In my own case, I spent eight years as a lay practitioner before I was ordained. I started practicing in the late sixties, and I had very independent ideas about what practice was. I figured that if the Buddha could realize himself without a teacher, I could do that also. I read books and I sat. After a while, lots of things began to surface in my sittings, and I really felt lost. I began searching for a teacher and eventually started to study with a Rinzai Master. I was still a lay practitioner.

During that period of time, most of my sitting was done at home, although I occasionally visited the Monastery. I began to devise ways of practicing at home, ways of making my training fill each day as much as possible. We were living in an isolated area, on a farm in the country, miles from the nearest store. It was a very simple existence. We heated with coal and there was no hot water. There were just three of us — my wife, one child, and me. Since my wife was also involved in practice and my son was just an infant, it was easy to structure our household and life around practice. I was running my own business, a studio, and later worked on writing a book, so that I could really plan the day the way I wanted to.

We started every day with dawn zazen. We got up the same time that the residents got up at the monastery. I made a home practice audio tape with the recorded sounds of the Monastery. All I had to do after the alarm went off and I woke up was to reach over and start the tape, and the room would be filled with the sounds one hears in the monastery in the morning — the *jikido* ringing the wakeup bell, the han being struck. I would splash some water on my face, put on my robe, and begin zazen. We had a tiny room that had an altar, and we would go in there and sit. The jikido would hit the inkin three times, the sitting period would start, we would do zazen for thirty-five minutes, then two hits on the bell would end the period. Kinhin, the sound of the clappers, then we would sit the second period. I also had recordings of the sangha chanting, and we would chant with them, practicing liturgy. We ate oryoki breakfast in silence.

Part of each day was set aside for art practice, which in my case was photography. In the evenings, I read. Archery was my body practice and I did it with some regularity. The bulk of the day, of course, was dedicated to work practice. Since I was self-employed, and had my own business, I was able to define my livelihood. It was during that time that I was really able to look and see what work was. I was running an advertising company and a photo gallery and I found out, as I began to examine the morality of my work, that what advertising basically does is create a need where none exists. That is its whole point. I started to look at the things that I was selling and, as the business grew and became successful, I was able to be more selective about my clients. I stopped taking clients in the fashion world, for example, because I felt that often, the only major difference between a three-hundred dollar dress and a fifty-dollar dress was some high-priced designer's name. For the most part, the materials and its production were the same. There were a few clients whose products were extraordinary. There was a furniture maker who made exquisite, hand-crafted pieces. I continued with him. I dropped an arms manufacturer. I began to pay attention to how my clients were nourishing the world. With time, it became more and more evident what I needed to do, and the shifts and adjustments continued.

Home practice evolved into a very strong, all-encompassing way of practicing. It felt just as strong as what was going on in the Monastery. I couldn't live in the Monastery because I had a wife and a child, and children were not allowed there. So I decided, "Okay, if the Monastery won't let me be there, I'll take the Monastery and bring it here." The only thing that I could not bring to my house was the teacher. So, several evenings each week I would go to the Monastery to do dokusan. Each month I would attend sesshin. This range of activity effectively made the Dharma the central focus of my life.

In setting up your own home practice, the first thing you need to do is to closely examine your circumstances and really be honest about your priorities. Be realistic. Everybody has responsibilities — paying the rent, maintaining a job, taking care of a family. Specifically, if you have children, they are your number one priority. They have no alternative to you. You have to take care of them, which means not only attending to their immediate needs, but creating a nurturing, loving environment for their growth. In the sixties and the seventies, I experienced first-hand what I call "spiritual orphans." These children reminded me of kids I'd seen in Italy in the days after World War II. Groups of six- to ten-year-olds lived in demolished, bombed out houses, and ran the streets like packs of wolves. The look on their faces was the same look I saw on the faces of the spiritual orphans whose parents were off "getting enlightened." These children were abandoned and had no adult supervision or models. To be a parent and to allow this to happen is not only not Dharma, it is also immoral. We have the ultimate responsibility to take care of the children we have brought into this world. The other side of that is that parents who are practicing, who are really working on themselves, usually turn out to be better, more sensitive parents. But no one should withdraw into and hide in practice at the expense of taking care of their duties.

After determining your priorities, you need to look at the possibilities of your practice. There are certain things that you can and cannot do based on where you live. For example, if you want to get up at four o'clock in the morning and chant Mu at the top of your lungs, and you live in an apartment with thin walls, your neighbors are not going to like that. So, that is not one of your possibilities. If you are convinced that ocean swimming is great body practice, but you live in the desert: reconsider. Taking one of your meals during the day in the formal oryoki style may be a wonderful practice, but if your mate who is present during this time is not a practitioner, trying to get them involved in it becomes the worst kind of evangelism. Keep your practice your own. To flaunt it, to sell it to others, only creates problems. Look at your relationships, your neighbors, your neighborhood, your household, and figure out what things are possible and what things are impractical in terms of pursuing your practice.

Then, the essential step is to create a special space for zazen. That space has a lot of importance. It can be a corner of a room, a closet, a whole room if that is available. It can even be an outdoor place, a clearing in the woods, if need be. That space should be your sacred space. It should feel right and powerful to you, as the place where you sit. Set up an altar there, with a Buddha image, and offer incense before doing zazen. Treat it in a sacred way. As you begin dealing with it and treating it in a special way, that attitude begins to open outward, and you start to treat everything that way. It is all sacred. Sacred and secular are not separated. Start at a particular point of focus, and allow it to expand to all aspects of your life.

It is a good idea to put on your robe when you are going to sit. Make sitting zazen a very conscious thing that you are doing. And remember that the length of time you sit is not as significant as continuity. It is much more important to sit ten minutes a day, every day, than to sit two hours once a week. If you are doing dawn zazen, ten minutes each day opens up the day for you, begins each day in a clear way. How long one sits varies for different practitioners. Whatever you decide to do, make sure that it is a schedule you can maintain, or you will find yourself cutting back on it, getting discouraged, and then stopping altogether. When you notice that happening, what you can do to help yourself is to plug into the sangha, to be recharged and get going again.

Dawn and evening are good times for zazen, as there are fewer distractions. If you have children, it is a good idea to do your zazen before your children are awake and after they have gone to bed for the night. Get up ten minutes, or half an hour earlier than you would normally, and use the extra time to start the day with sitting. Splash some water on your face, have a cup of tea, wake up, and then do dawn zazen. This is also a good way to close out the day.

Regular morning and evening zazen are an excellent way to anchor your practice, but sometimes it is simply impossible to work out your schedule that way. During a period of time when I was the director of an art museum, we had twelve employees, operated two galleries, offered classes at several studios, and were open every day from eight o'clock in the morning till nine o'clock at night. To keep continuity in my sitting, I would go into one of the empty studios and do my zazen in the middle of the afternoon. It was a great way to carry my practice through the day.

One day, one of the people accidentally walked into the room where I was sitting. Soon the place was buzzing with questions: I was a closet Buddhist and they had no idea what I was doing. A couple of the more assertive employees wanted to know what my sitting was all about. I explained, and suddenly they were all interested and listening, and wanted to learn how to do it. One thing led to another, and within two or three months, the entire group was doing zazen in the afternoon. We would close the door, put out the "out to lunch" sign, and we would sit together. Then, we began evening zazen, and morning zazen before we started working, so we were doing zazen three times a day. Several artists who were teaching courses began their classes with ten minutes of zazen. It is amazing to see how one's own personal zazen reaches out and touches everything that is around, in ways that sometimes one is not even aware of. It is a vital matter not to lose touch with your zazen.

Although zazen is the cornerstone of our practice both at home and at the Monastery, all eight areas of training have to be actively cultivated for this practice to fully unfold. Zazen is the most directly visible and accessible aspect of the training. The teacher-student relationship poses more difficult problems. My availability to people who live far away from the Monastery or who cannot travel to see me is a real limitation. But keep in mind that the teacher-student relationship does not exclusively happen with respect to the physical entity of this teacher. The relationship extends to all the teachers in this lineage. This teacher represents the successive generations of ancestors, from Shakyamuni Buddha, right down to this time and this place. If you are aware of that fact, you can access the teacher-student relationship in many ways. You can plug into that lineage just by chanting the names of the ancestors. You can become intimate with the teachers by wholeheartedly studying their teachings.

The teacher-student relationship in Zen is not a devotional practice. It is not a guru worship. But, at the same time, we consciously acknowledge our connection to the past teachers, our gratitude to them, our common identity. In the Buddha Hall at the Monastery, up on the altar, there are photos of the most recent teachers of our lineage — my own teacher, Maezumi Roshi, and his teachers Kuroda Roshi, Yasutani Roshi and Koryu Roshi. Each morning there is a service in that Buddha Hall that connects me to those four people and their teachings, even though I have never met three of them. The physical meeting never happened but that does not exclude the possibility of genuine intimacy with these masters.

Correspondence with a teacher is another way of keeping the edge of the relationship active, although, in my case, I am not a great letter writer. Nevertheless, I have observed throughout the years, that in approaching one's questions seriously and in depth, one generates the appropriate answers. I see this repeatedly while working with students in dokusan. I usually don't say much during dokusan. You do most of the work as you sit on the dokusan line and sweat with your questions. When you come in, you have to present yourself so that I can understand it, and in the process of doing that, by the time you are saying it to me, I can see on your face that the answer is really clear, and I don't have to do anything more than grunt or say "I don't know," ring the bell and the whole matter is taken care of. So, in corresponding with students, I find that I don't have to write long letters and respond with intellectual explanations or advice. When I receive an involved letter from a student, in most cases, right in the struggle of that letter I see the response. I answer briefly, cut out and paste the appropriate part of the original letter, and put a big red arrow pointing to it with "here's your answer."

For academic study, the training office at the Monastery provides a reading list for each of the ten stages of training. (See Appendix.) Most people approach academic study, the reading of the ancient and modern texts, incorrectly. When I recommend that you should study the *Diamond Sutra*, I do not mean that you should read it overnight. Although it is a thin book, you cannot read the *Diamond Sutra* in one sitting. The *Diamond Sutra* needs to be chewed paragraph by paragraph, over and over. Its language is archaic and it is very repetitive. It is easy to get bored with it and stop hearing it. It has to be read slowly and contemplatively. Most of the sutras are that way, all of the koans are that way. Ideally, proper academic study calls for a period of time that is preceded by zazen, where you can really give yourself to the writings with your whole body and mind. You must digest it and assimilate it with every cell of your body. It is not study for an examination — it is for your life.

It is very relevant for Westerners to become more familiar with Buddhist history, philosophy, and psychology, by taking courses at local universities, if such are available, or by reading scholarly books. Our understanding of the process can be enhanced by our understanding of the context. It is also acceptable to take advantage of studying with other teachers who are more accessible, but do take care to see that they are legitimate masters, sanctioned by their own teachers.

I suggest that you do morning and evening liturgy at home. Keep it simple. Whether you have received the Precepts or not, chant the *Verse of the Kesa* as a way of ending your dawn sitting. At some time in the morning, do the *Heart Sutra.* It is a wonderful way to refresh oneself each day. In the evening, chant the *Four Vows.* These are the vows of all Mahayana Buddhists — to save all sentient beings. Chanting the *Evening Gatha* before retiring for the night reminds you of the preciousness of your life and the commitment you have to your practice.

The most important aspect of the practice of the Precepts is to repeatedly recall what they are, and to see the places where they emerge into the light of your life. The Six Paramitas — *dana, sila, ksanti, prajna, virya,* and *dhyana* — are another doorway to the practice of the Precepts. They are definitely a worthwhile study, having to do with Buddhism's moral and ethical teachings. Dana is giving and generosity. Sila is morality, the actual functioning of the Precepts. Ksanti is patience. Prajna paramita is the "wisdom of the other shore." Patience is one of the more important aspects of that wisdom. Virya is energy or exertion. It is *ki*, self empowerment. Dhyana paramita is your zazen.

If you have an art practice that you normally do, it is good to continue that practice, but also to keep in mind that your art may benefit from in-depth exploration of one of the traditional Zen arts — flower arranging, calligraphy, shakuhachi, *sumi-e* painting — whatever relates to your field. If it is music, then shakuhachi is a good instrument to study. If it is drama, then Noh drama might be appropriate. If it is literary arts, haiku could expand your vistas. If it is western graphics, eastern calligraphy would be worth looking at. If your art work is one-sided, embedded within a stale context, what practicing Zen arts does is to spark a different way of seeing, perceiving and creating with a different kind of aesthetic. This aesthetic then begins to manifest itself in the western art forms, and in your life.

As in other areas of training, consistency is key to body practice. A routine that alternates between art practice and body practice every other day, with one day off during the week, is often both feasible and reasonable. Body practice can be anything from jogging to swimming to martial arts to archery. If you have the opportunity to study one of the martial arts, you will get to see some of the Zen principles that have emerged from the ancient Shao-lin monastery in China, and that are equally applicable to any form of body practice. In doing a body practice, always work from the hara, starting with the stillness of zazen. Have that stillness open up into every activity of the body, and then end the activity by returning to that still point of zazen.

There are some traditional martial arts masters who are truly excellent teachers, especially when they are also seasoned Zen practitioners. To study with such people is a unique and wonderful experience. Though many people talk about the spiritual basis of the martial arts, very few really practice it. What one usually gets is a lot of flashy lip service, flexed muscles, and macho attitude. A genuine master's spirituality will come through in the way he shakes hands and the way he is loving and open to the people he is working with. Instead of posturing, there is an embodiment of gentleness and compassion.

Work practice is the biggest leap. It is relatively easy to see how to lift a cup of tea mindfully, or how to make a brush stroke from the hara. Once you get out into the world, however, and are struggling with people who don't care that you are a Buddhist being mindful, the whole thing can get crazy. The entire practice, right down to its very foundation, is really tested.

The first thing you need to look at in your work practice is how you make your living. Put any doubts and persistent conflicts to rest. In our sangha there is an environmental lawyer. She started practicing and became a student about five years ago. She is very bright. She was working for a huge law firm, making lots of money, but was very unhappy. She felt that what she was doing was inconsistent with her practice. She didn't like the cases she was involved in. Her heart wasn't in it. She wanted to know what to do. I said "Quit!" And she said "Quit?!" She was very conservative, not aggressive at all. I said "Yeah, quit. Leave it, start your own little firm. You don't need to work for anyone else." She said "Oh, I don't know if I could do that..." This went on for about a year in dokusan. It became her koan. She would come in and she'd complain about what she was doing and I'd say "Quit!" So, one day she did it. She quit her job and started her own law firm. For the next year that's all I heard about — "Oh, it's not going to work... I can't pay the rent..." Five years later, this person has one of the best small environmental law firms in the country. Several of her clients are mayors of major cities. She goes to Washington as an environmental advisor for Congress. She has several lawyers working for her. She travels to Eastern Europe because they have environmental concerns. She is more content and at peace with herself. She is doing right livelihood; she is *being* ecology, which is what she wanted. All it took to make the shift was looking long and hard enough at her discomfort to realize that she could do what she needed to do.

There are certain things we each can do; we don't need to do them the way everyone else in society is doing them. We can shift, we can adapt, we can transform. We can take the hours of labor that we have in us for the rest of our lives and turn them into good for other beings, all other sentient beings, and make a living to boot. Everyone of us, regardless of what our livelihood is and what are our talents are, has that capacity. Some of you have already looked at it and have shifted things as necessary. Others of you are still considering it. Have patience — you don't have to rush it. All you need to do in life to really get things to happen is to be aware. The simplicity and force of such attention is amazing. You don't need to write a five-year plan of what you are going to do: just keep your awareness on what you are doing. You will be surprised how things will change for you. Energy will come pouring into it. That is the way this sangha started, that is the way it is developing, that is the way it is going to continue. It will grow just by our own practice and awareness. The things that we need will come when the time is right. If we practice, if our intention is good, not self-serving but for the benefit of all sentient beings, it will happen.

In Zen training, we talk about "ascending the mountain practice" and "descending the mountain practice." Ascending the mountain is renouncing the world and single-mindedly dedicating yourself to the practice. When you finally reach the mountain peak and realize yourself, you have to come down and go back into the world, to manifest what has been realized in everything that you do. Lay practice, home practice, always takes place as descending the mountain training. You always do it in the world, in the midst of samsara. We call it "the lotus in the fire." The lotus is the symbol of enlightenment. Many images of the Buddha show him sitting upon a huge lotus flower. We chant at the end of oryoki, "May we exist in muddy water with purity like the lotus, thus we bow to Buddha." The interesting thing about the lotus is that if you took it and planted it in pure water, it would die. It can't live in purity. It can only live in decay and mud and things breaking down. That is our practice — samsara *is* nirvana. Samsara is necessary for nirvana; they are co-dependent entities. In the middle of the fire of samsara, the lotus grows. In the midst of the fire of greed, anger, and ignorance of the world, the lotus blooms. That is your practice. That is home practice. It may seem like a tremendous and endless disadvantage, but it is a priceless gift. The fire burns, the lotus blooms. Indeed, it is *because* the fire burns that the lotus can bloom.

HOMELEAVING

While developing the collection of *Koans of the Way of Reality* over the past several years, I have tried to bring together koans that are of particular relevance to Western practitioners. One of the areas of concern is the relationship between monk practice and lay practice. Ultimately, the choice of whether to follow the route of a monk or a lay practitioner is something only each individual can decide. Even after one has decided, it may not be possible, due to individual karma, to actually take the course of action one feels drawn to. Obviously, this is not the kind of a question that can be resolved abstractly; any decision about the course of one's practice has to stem from individual inclinations and circumstances.

Several cases in *Koans of the Way of Reality* that focus on lay practice derive from the *Vimalakirti Sutra*. I have also used the P'ang family as a source of koans on lay practice. There is, as well, a series of koans specifically about monk practice. The koan on Upagupta's enlightenment is an attempt to bring monk and lay practice together.

The heart and essence of Buddha's teaching is in the action of homeleaving. Yet homeleaving is not a function of body or mind. The cause and effect of homeleaving and enlightenment are one reality. One does not precede the other. Supreme enlightenment is realized the moment there is homeleaving. At the moment of supreme enlightenment, not only does homeleaving occur, but the house itself disintegrates and the self perishes. Raising the bodhi mind, homeleaving, and enlightenment are not three. They are not actions bound by time or space, but rather exist amid endless eons of time and boundless universes of space. All attachments are cut free, body and mind fall away. Homeleaving is just this — nothing further. It is not like something.

The above prologue points to what it is about: "The heart and essence of Buddha's teaching is in the action of homeleaving." Homeleaving is *shukke-tokudo*, or renunciation of the world. Normally, "homeleaving" is the term used to describe what a student does when he or she enters into the monkhood, literally leaving their home and family. But homeleaving can be understood on many levels, and that is what I want to investigate here.

"Homeleaving," the koan says, "is not a function of body or mind." It is not something you do with your mind; it is not something you do with your body. "The cause and effect of homeleaving and enlightenment are one reality." In other words, to leave home is enlightenment. Enlightenment is to leave home. "One does not precede the other. Supreme enlightenment is realized the moment there is homeleaving. And at the moment of supreme enlightenment, not only does homeleaving occur, but the house itself disintegrates, and the self perishes." We should look closely here at what is meant by homeleaving.

"Raising the bodhi mind, homeleaving, and enlightenment," — in other words, the aspiration for enlightenment, leaving home, and enlightenment itself — are not three separate things. "They are not actions that are bound by time or space, but rather exist amid the endless eons of time and the boundless universes of space." This says that homeleaving is omnipresent, always present. It does not have to do with a particular point in time. It is part of the continuum we call practice. Your realization is the realization of the Buddha. Your realization confirms and actualizes the realization of all of the Buddhas and ancestors from time immemorial. "All attachments are cut free, body and mind fall away. Homeleaving is just this — nothing further." The homeleaving being referred to is the cutting away of all attachments. "It's not *like* something." There is nothing to compare it to. It has no reference system. It is absolute.

The main body of this koan states:

Once the venerable Shanavasa asked Upagupta, "Did you make your home departure physically, or in spirit?" Upagupta replied, "Truly, I made my home departure physically." Shanavasa said, "How can the wondrous Dharma of the Buddhas have anything to do with body or mind?" On hearing this, Upagupta was greatly awakened.

Upagupta first visited Shanavasa at the age of 15. At the age of 17 he was ordained, thus making his home departure, and became Shanavasa's attendant. At 22, he realized himself. When Shanavasa asked, "Did you make your home departure physically, or spiritually?" he was referring to a distinction made at times in Buddhism between two kinds of home departure, one physical, the other mental. Leaving home physically means that one casts away all worldly things: relationships, affections, one's house. A monk shaves his or her head, puts on monk's robes, takes a vow of poverty, of service, of simplicity, and makes an effort to realize the Way through the twenty-four hours of each day. "Whatever the time," Keizan Zenji says, "monks do not pass it in vain. They desire nothing else. Therefore, they neither delight in life nor fear death. Their minds are as pure as the autumn moon, their eyes as clear as a bright mirror. They do not seek mind, nor do they hanker to see their original natures. They do not cultivate the holy truth, much less worldly attachments. In this way, they do not abide in the stage of ordinary persons, nor cherish the rank of the wise and holy, but more and more become mindless seekers of the Way." These are the people who leave home physically.

Keizan says, "Then there are those that leave home mentally or in spirit. They don't shave their heads, nor wear monk's clothing. But even though they live at home, and remain among worldly cares, they are like lotuses, which are not soiled by the mud in which they grow, or like jewels, which are immune to contamination by dust. Even though there are karmic conditions, so that they have spouses, or children, they consider them without attachment. They do not covet anything, like the moon suspended in the sky. Like a ball rolling on a tray, they live in a noisy city, and see the one who is leisurely in the three times of past, future, and present. They clarify the fact that they are timeless, they realize that exterminating the passions is a sickness, and that aiming for ultimate reality is wrong. Both nirvana and samsara are illusions, and they are not attached to either enlightenment or the passions." These are lay practitioners who leave home in spirit.

Shanavasa wanted to know what kind of homeleaving Upagupta made. Was it physical or was it in spirit? If it is not one, it must be the other. If it is not one or the other, then it is not home departure. When Upagupta responded that he had left home physically, he was referring to his taking the vows of a monk, shaving his head and putting on monk robes. But the master was coming from the standpoint of the Buddha's wondrous Dharma. The Buddha did not leave home physically, nor did he leave home mentally, in spirit. Homeleaving should not be understood in terms of the "four elements and five aggregates," that is, the body and mind. It should not even be seen as the profound mystery of truth.

Keizan Zenji says, "It is like vast space, neither inside nor outside. When one realizes oneself, one transcends birth and death. One is liberated from mind and no-mind. It is like water conforming to its container. Like space which rests against things. Though you grasp it, your hands are not filled. Though you search for it, you can't find a trace of it." This is the Dharma of the Buddha. When you reach this place, there is no Upagupta or Shanavasa. It has nothing to do with coming or going. Even though there is "is" and "is not," Keizan says, "it is like the sound at the bottom of a stream, or like endless space."

To the main case I've added the following footnotes. *Once the venerable Shanavasa asked Upagupta.* The footnote says, "It's necessary to pose the question. He must test the man." This is a very interesting part of our training, and it is unlike religious training in general. In Catholic monasticism, as well as in most of forms of Buddhism, there is little actual testing that goes on. But in Zen, because the major thrust of practice is to realize oneself, there is often this probing. Whether it be gradual or sudden, the ultimate function of shikantaza or koan introspection is the realization of oneself.

In dokusan, the face-to-face teaching, there is usually probing, of the student and of the teacher. The same testing functions in public Dharma Combat, and in Shuso Hossen. The shuso or head seminarian is selected from among the most senior of the junior students, and for a period of ninety days, becomes the model of their particular kind of practice, either lay or monk. At the end of those ninety days, the shuso is empowered by the teacher, signified by the handing over of the *sheppei*. The sheppei is a broken bow that the teacher received from his or her teacher during the transmission ceremony. The shuso then presents a Dharma talk and challenges the sangha: "Now you dragons and elephants in this Dharma hall, confront me in Dharma Combat!" The shuso is saying, "Test me!" The students then pose questions, examining the understanding of the shuso. The shuso responds and dialogues ensue. In this way, the sangha approves the new shuso. It is not just a matter of the teacher empowering the student, or of the shuso empowering him or herself, but it is also an empowerment by the sangha. Everything we do is the Three Treasures: Buddha, Dharma, Sangha. Generation after generation, this testing is what keeps our practice alive and hopping. Otherwise, it would become very stale and dull.

For the next line, *Did you make your home departure physically, or in spirit?* the footnote says, "Iron brambles — there are many that have questions about this." The forest of brambles is made of thickets and intertwining vines. It is very difficult to pass through. You have to hack every foot of the way. Those brambles are all the things we cling to, all of the barriers we encounter in our life — the difficulties, pain, and struggles. You have to make your way through the forest of brambles to realize yourself. Now, this venerable old master creates a forest of *iron* brambles. Is your home departure made physically or in spirit? The same question has come up hundreds of times in this sangha. What does home departure mean? What does being a monk mean?

Upagupta replied, "Truly, I made my home departure physically." The footnote says, "What is he saying? He sure isn't alert. This monk's body is cut in half." This refers to the duality the monk is stuck in. Many of the koans deal with dualities. Dualities come up in a hundred billion forms. We seem to resolve one, only to become entangled in another. Cause and effect: duality. Enlightenment and delusion: duality. Good and evil: duality. Male and female: duality. Heaven and earth: duality. Physically or mentally: duality. Pick one of them. "Physically," Upagupta says. And when he says that, he cuts himself into pieces. He puts mental in one pocket and physical in another. Spiritual on one side, mundane on the other. "In the world" on one side, "on the mountain" on the other side. The Dharma is not like that. How do you unite it? What is the truth that falls into neither side, that is neither absolute nor relative?

The master said, "How can the wondrous Dharma of the Buddhas have anything to do with body or mind?" The footnote says, "The universe is boundless; adepts are few. The ten directions cannot hold it. When the universe crumbles, it is not destroyed." This wondrous Dharma of the Buddhas is boundless, without edges. When you make body and mind, you chop it up. That is why it is said, "When the universe is destroyed, *it* is not destroyed."

On hearing this, Upagupta was greatly awakened. The footnote says, "Among the dead, one comes to life. He's now treading on the ground of reality. But tell me, awakened to what?" What is it that he saw? Don't give me a description of this reality, show me the reality itself. What this venerable old master was pointing to here is realization itself. What the prologue is pointing to is realization itself. That is, realizing one's inherent nature. This is not something that one acquires. It is not something that is transmitted. What is transmitted by Buddhas and ancestors is *not* inherent nature.

Even if the Buddhadharma died out from the face of the earth for 1,000 years, as was predicted by the Buddha, if there was not a sutra to be found, not a word of the Dharma, a Buddha image, or a teacher, just one person realizing themselves *immediately* connects back to the unbroken continuum of mind-to-mind transmission. But how could it be unbroken if there were 1,000 years in between? Inherent nature was never lost in those 1,000 years. It was always there. Buddha nature was always there. It just wasn't realized. Some may realize it, some may not. But that doesn't mean that it is not there.

Under all of our conditioning is the ground of being, the Buddha nature. What most of our practice is about, from the first through the tenth stage, is actually deconditioning, kensho notwithstanding. Seeing the nature of the self takes place in what we call stage three or four of practice, but that is just a step along the way. Seeing it is one thing, manifesting it is another. The third ox-herding picture, in which the ox, the self-nature, is first glimpsed, is a long way from the end of the journey. The ox must be taken hold of, then tamed. It takes time. We may have all kinds of wonderful ideas about wisdom and compassion, but somehow, body and mind just go merrily on their way following the program. We all vow to be compassionate, all things are one. Still there are moments of "But I can't stand that bastard!"

All the devices of the Eight Gates used in training — zazen, koans, liturgy, Shuso Hossen, mondo, dokusan, art practice, body practice, oryoki — directly point to the inherent nature underneath our conditioning. That's the unbroken lineage. When you realize it, you plug into the truth that has been realized by all the Buddhas and ancestors since time immemorial. Before there ever was a Buddha, there was Buddha nature. Long after there was a Buddha, there will be Buddha nature. When the universe is utterly and completely destroyed, there will be Buddha nature. People somehow worry about statements like, "Not only does homeleaving occur, but the house itself disintegrates, and the self perishes." But the "house itself" is the set of constructs we have built with our discriminating minds.

One of the purposes of koan study and practice is to take out the nails, kick out the wedges, and collapse the structure. The self perishes. Self is forgotten. What is the self that we so tenaciously hold on to? We worry about non-attachment, and have all kinds of ideas about it. Non-attachment is not about not caring, or not loving, or not doing. It is just non-attachment. Not holding on. Not attempting to control and to manipulate. Not sticking. Body and mind fallen away is not zombie-land. Self forgotten is not a dead person walking. It is alive and vital, functioning freely. What is yourself? Is it body? Is it mind? Is it neither body nor mind? Is it both body and mind? Self is an idea. It does not exist. We create it, moment to moment to moment. Whatever we hold on to creates a self. That is why the process of deconditioning takes so long. It is not until we are really free of our attachments that we realize the complete falling away of body and mind. The true self. The ground of reality.

There is a capping verse to this koan.

The one great pearl is always present.
Dragon sons and daughters
Are always born of dragon parents.
But how can it be spoken of?
The rains have passed,
And the autumn river runs deep and fast.

The one great pearl is another expression for the true Dharma eye, the eye of reality, the Way, the Buddha nature, inherent nature. It is always present. It is not something that can be given or received. It cannot be acquired. "Dragon sons and daughters are always born of dragon parents." Dragons are enlightened beings. Buddhas only transmit to Buddhas. Buddhahood can only be realized by Buddhas. But the question is, how can it be spoken of? What can be said about it? "The rains have passed, and the autumn river runs deep and fast." The wind blows from the west, leaves gather in the east. When it rains, you open an umbrella. If you don't have an umbrella, your head gets wet. So simple, and yet so complicated. It takes a lot of conditioning to separate us from our true nature. We spend a lifetime doing it. It takes a lot of training to reconnect us with our true nature.

There is a moment when we realize that something is not quite right, that we somehow have not been given the whole story, that there is something more to this life than what people seem to think, or what we've been told. The moment that thought arises, we have done what is called "raising the bodhi mind," the aspiration for enlightenment. The moment you do that, the moment that happens, the whole process is complete. This is a process beyond time and space. And it is the birth potential of all sentient beings. Many will not do it, many will. But for those of us who have entered the Way, and by that I mean simply to have placed your body in the meditative posture, it is hard to turn back. If you just forget about when, how much, how fast am I moving, what rank am I, who's better than me, who am I better than... throw all those things away, then there is just practice, moment to moment. Not only that which takes place on a zafu, but in the twenty-four hours of each day, in every aspect of our life. That is when practice has really come home. That is the Nirmanakaya, the body of the Buddha — *your* body.

APPENDICES

MASTER DOGEN'S
MOUNTAINS AND RIVERS SUTRA

These mountains and rivers of the present are the actualization of the word of the ancient Buddhas. Each, abiding in (its own) dharma state, completely fulfills its virtues. Because they are the state prior to the *kalpa* of emptiness, they are living in the present. Because they are the self before the germination of any subtle sign, they are liberated in their actualization.

Because the virtues of the mountains are high and broad, the power to ride the clouds is always penetrated from the mountains; and the ability to follow the wind is inevitably liberated from the mountains.

Master Ta-Yang Shan-K'ai addressed the assembly: "The blue mountains are constantly walking. The stone woman gives birth to a child in the night." The mountains lack none of their proper virtues; hence, they are constantly at rest and constantly walking. We must devote ourselves to a detailed study of this virtue of walking. The walking of the mountains is like that of men: do not doubt that the mountains walk simply because they may not appear to walk like humans. These words of the Ancestor (Ta-Yang) point out the fundamental meaning of walking, and we should thoroughly investigate his teaching on "constant walking."

Because (the blue mountains) are walking they are constant. Their walk is swifter than the wind; yet those in the mountains do not sense this, do not know it. To be "in the mountains" is a flower opening "within the world." Those outside the mountains do not sense this, do not know it. Those without eyes to see the mountains do not sense, do not know, do not see, do not hear this truth.

They who doubt that the mountains walk do not yet understand their own walking. It is not that they do not walk, but that they do not yet understand, have not made clear, walking itself. They who would understand their own walking must also understand the walking of the blue mountains. The blue mountains are neither sentient nor insentient; the self is neither sentient nor insentient. Therefore, we can have no doubts about these blue mountains walking.

We do not realize that we must clarify the blue mountains on the basis of innumerable dharma realms. We must carefully investigate the walking of the blue mountains, the walking of the self. And this investigation should include walking backward as well as backward walking. We should carefully investigate the fact that since that very time before any subtle sign, since the age of the King of Emptiness, walking both forward and backward has never stopped for a moment. If walking had ever rested, the Buddhas and Ancestors would never have appeared; if walking were limited, the Buddhadharma would never have reached the present. Walking forward has never ceased; walking backward has never ceased. Walking forward does not oppose walking backward, nor does walking backward oppose walking forward. This virtue is called "the mountain flowing, the flowing mountain."

The blue mountains devote themselves to the investigation of walking; the East Mountain devotes itself to the study of "moving over the water." Hence, this study is the mountains' own study. The mountains, unchanged in body and mind, maintaining their own mountain countenance, have always been traveling about studying themselves. Do not slight mountains by saying that the blue mountains cannot walk, nor the East Mountain move over the water. It is because of the impoverishment of the common point of view that we doubt the statement, "the blue mountains walk"; it is because of the shallowness of our limited experience that we are surprised by the words, "flowing mountain." Without having fully understood even the words, "flowing water," we simply remain sunk in ordinary perception.

Thus, the accumulated virtues (of the mountain) represent its name and form, its very lifeblood. There is a mountain walk and a mountain flow, and there is a time when the mountain gives birth to a mountain child. The mountains become the Buddhas and Ancestors, and it is for this reason that the Buddhas and Ancestors have thus appeared.

Even when we have the eyes (to see mountains as) the appearance of grass and trees, earth and stone, fences and walls, this is nothing to doubt, nothing to be moved by: it is not the complete actualization (of the mountains). Even when there occurs a time in which (the mountains) are perceived as the splendor of the seven treasures, this is still not the real refuge. Even when (the mountains) appear as the realm of the practice of the Buddhas, this is not necessarily something to be desired. Even when we attain the supreme (vision) of (the mountains as) the actualization of the inconceivable virtue of the Buddhas, this is not yet the complete reality. Each of these appearances is the particular objective and subjective reward (of past karma). They are not the karma of the way of the Buddhas and Ancestors, but narrow, one-sided views.

Turning the object and turning the mind is criticized by the Great Sage; explaining the mind and explaining the nature is not affirmed by the Buddhas and Ancestors; seeing the mind and seeing the nature is the business of non-Buddhists: sticking to words and sticking to phrases is not the speech of liberation. There is (speech) which is free from such realms; it is "the blue mountains constantly walking," "the East Mountain moving over the water." We should give this detailed investigation.

"The stone woman gives birth to a child in the night." This means that the time when "the stone woman gives birth to a child" is the "night." Among stones there are male stones, female stones, and stones neither male nor female. These stones give support to heaven and to earth. There are heavenly stones and earthly stones. Although this is said in the secular world, it is rarely understood. We should understand the true nature of the "birth." At the time of birth are both parent and child transformed? We must study and fully understand, not only that birth is actualized in the child becoming the parent, but also that the practice and verification of the phenomenon of birth occurs when the parent becomes the child.

The great Master Yun-men K'uang-chen has said, "The East Mountain moves over the water." The import of this expression is that all mountains are the East Mountain, and all these East Mountains are moving over the water. Therefore, Mount Sumeru and the other nine mountains are all actualizing themselves, are all practicing and verifying (the Buddhadharma). This is called "the East Mountain." But is Yun-men himself liberated from skin, flesh, bones, and marrow of the East Mountain and its life of practice and verification?

At the present time in the land of Sung there is a certain crude bunch who have by now formed such a crowd that they cannot be overcome by the few true (students of the Way). They maintain that talk such as this "East Mountain moving over the water" or Nan-ch'uan's "sickle" is incomprehensible. Their idea is that any talk which can be grasped by thought is not the Zen talk of the Buddhas and Ancestors; indeed, it is precisely incomprehensible talk that is the talk of the Buddhas and Ancestors. Consequently, they hold that Huang-po's stick and Lin-chi's roar, because they cannot be comprehended or grasped by thought, represent that great awakening preceding the time before the germination of any subtle sign. The "tangle-cutting words" often used as teaching devices by the great masters of the past are impossible (they say) to comprehend.

Those who talk in this way have never met a true teacher, and lack the eye of study. What they call "incomprehensible talk" is incomprehensible only to them, not to the Buddhas and Ancestors. Simply because they themselves do not comprehend it is no reason for them not to study the way the Buddhas and Ancestors comprehend. Even granted that it was incomprehensible, it would then follow that this comprehension they now seek to maintain must also be wrong.

Such people are common throughout Sung China, and I have seen them with my own eyes. They do not know that thought is words; they do not know that words are liberated from thought.

We should realize that this (teaching of) "the East Mountain moving over the water" is the very bones and marrow of the Buddhas and Ancestors. All the waters are appearing at the foot of the East Mountain; and therefore, the mountains mount the clouds and stride through the heavens. The mountains are the peaks of the waters, and in both ascending and descending their walk is "over the water." The tips of the mountains' feet walk across the waters, setting them dancing; therefore, walking extends freely in all directions, and "practice and verification are not nonexistent."

Water is neither strong nor weak, neither wet nor dry, neither moving nor still, neither cold nor hot, neither being nor nonbeing, neither delusion nor enlightenment. Solidified, it is harder than diamond: who could break it? Melted, it is softer than milk: who could break it? This being the case, we cannot doubt the many virtues realized (by water). We should, then, study that occasion when the water of the ten directions is seen in the ten directions. This is not a study only of the time when people or Gods see water: there is a study of water seeing water. Water practices and verifies water; hence, there is a study of water speaking water. We must bring to realization the path on which the self encounters the self. We must move back and forth along, and spring off from, the vital path on which the other studies and fully comprehends the other.

In general, then, the way of seeing mountains and rivers differs according to the type of being (that sees them). There are beings who see what we call water as a jeweled necklace. This does not mean, however, that they see a jeweled necklace as water. How, then, do we see what they consider water? Their jeweled necklace is what we see as water. Or, again they see water as miraculous flowers, though it does not follow that they use flowers as water. Hungry ghosts see water as raging flames or as pus and blood. Dragons and fish see it as a palace or a tower, or as the seven treasures or the *mani* gem. (Others) see (water) as woods and walls, or as the dharma nature of immaculate liberation, or as the true human body, or as the physical form and mental nature. Men see these as water. And these (different ways of seeing) are the conditions under which (water) is killed or given life.

Thus, what different types of beings see is different; and we should reflect on this fact. Is it that there are various ways of seeing one object? Or is it that we have mistaken various images for one object? We should concentrate every effort on understanding this question, and then concentrate still more. Given this (multitude of perspectives), it follows that the training on the way of practice and verification must also not be merely of one or two kinds, and the ultimate realm must also have a thousand types and ten thousand kinds.

If we reflect on the real import of this (problem), although we say there are many types of water, it would seem there is no original water, no water of various types. Nevertheless, the waters which vary in accordance with the different types of beings do not depend on body or mind; they do not arise from karma; they are not dependent on the self or the other: dependent on water, (water) is liberated.

Therefore, water is not earth, water, fire, wind, space, or consciousness; it is not blue, yellow, red, white, or black; it is not form, sound, smell, taste, touch, or idea: nevertheless, the water of earth, water, fire, wind, space, and the rest is spontaneously appearing. This being the case, it becomes difficult to explain by what and of what this present land and palace are made. To say that they rest on the wheel of space and the wheel of wind is true neither for oneself nor for others; it is just speculating on the basis of the suppositions of little understanding, and is only said out of fear that without such resting place (things) would not abide.

The Buddha has said, "All dharmas are ultimately liberated; they have no abode." We should realize that although they are liberated, without any bonds, all dharmas are abiding in (their own) state. However, when humans look at water they see it only as flowing without rest. This "flow" takes many forms, and our (way of seeing) is just a one-sided human view. Water flows over the earth; it flows across the sky; it flows up; it flows down. (Water) flows around bends and into deep abysses. It mounts up to form clouds; it descends to form pools.

The *Wen-tzu* says, "The tao of water, ascending to heaven becomes rain and dew, descending to earth becomes rivers and streams." Such is said even in the secular world. It would be shameful indeed if those who call themselves descendants of the Buddhas and Ancestors had less understanding than the ordinary person.

(This passage) says that, although the way of water is unknown to water, water actually functions (as water); and although the way of water is not unknown to water, water actually functions (as water).

"Ascending to heaven, it becomes rain and dew." We should realize that water climbs to the very highest heavens, and becomes rain and dew. And this rain and dew is of various kinds in accordance with the various worlds. To say that there are places to which water does not reach is the false doctrine of the non-Buddhist. Water extends into flames; it extends into thought, reasoning, and discrimination; it extends into enlightenment and the Buddha nature.

"Descending to earth, it becomes rivers and streams." We should realize that when water descends to earth it becomes rivers and streams. And the essence of rivers and streams becomes sages. Common people think that water is always in rivers, streams, and seas, but this is not so: (water) makes rivers and seas within water. Therefore, water is in places that are not rivers and seas; it is just that when water descends to earth it acts as rivers and seas.

Moreover, we should not think that when water has become rivers and seas there is then no world and no Buddha land (within water): even within a single drop of water incalculable Buddha realms are actualized. Consequently, it is not that water exists within the Buddha land, nor that the Buddha land exists within water: the existence of water has nothing whatever to do with the three times or the dharma realm. And yet, (water) is the koan of the actualization of water.

Wherever the Buddhas and Ancestors are, water is always there; wherever water is, there the Buddhas and Ancestors always appear. Therefore, the Buddhas and Ancestors have always taken up water as their own body and mind, their own thinking.

In this way, then, (the idea) that water does not climb up is to be found neither in Buddhist nor non-Buddhist writings. The way of water penetrates everywhere, above and below, vertically and horizontally. Still, in the sutras it is said that fire and wind go up, while earth and water go down. But this "up and down" bears some study—the study of the up and down of the way of the Buddha. (In Buddhism) where earth and water go is considered "down"; but "down" does not mean some place to which earth and water go. Where fire and wind go is "up." While the dharma realm has no necessary connection with up and down and the four directions, simply on the basis of the function of the four, five, or six elements we provisionally set up a dharma realm with directions. It is not that heaven is above and hell below: hell is the entire dharma realm; heaven is the entire dharma realm.

Nevertheless, when dragons and fish see water as a palace, just as humans see palaces, they do not view it as flowing. And if some onlooker were to explain to them that their palace was flowing water they would surely be just as amazed as we are now to hear it said that mountains flow. Still, there would undoubtedly be some (dragons and fish) who would accept such an explanation of the railings, stairs, and columns of palaces and pavilions. We should calmly consider over and over the reasons for this. If our study is not liberated from these confines, we have not freed ourselves from the body and mind of the ordinary person, we have not fully comprehended the land of the Buddhas and Ancestors; we have not fully comprehended the land of the ordinary person; we have not fully comprehended the palace of the ordinary person.

Although humans have understood what is in seas and rivers as water, just what kind of thing dragons, fish, and other beings understand and use as water we do not yet know. Do not foolishly assume that all kinds of beings must use as water what we understand as water. When those who study Buddhism seek to learn about water, they should not stick to (the water of) humans; they should go on to study the water of Buddhism. We should study how we see the water used by the Buddhas and Ancestors; we should study whether within the rooms of the Buddhas and Ancestors there is or is not water.

From time immemorial the mountains have been the dwelling place of the great sages; wise ones and sages have made the mountains their own chamber, their own body and mind. And through these wise ones and sages the mountains have been actualized. However many great sages and wise ones we suppose have assembled in the mountains, ever since they entered the mountains no one has met a single one of them. There is only the actualization of the life of the mountains; not a single trace of their having entered remains.

The countenance (of the mountains) is completely different when we are in the world gazing off at the mountains and when we are in the mountains meeting the mountains. Our consideration and our understanding of nonflowing should not be the same as the dragon's understanding. Humans and gods reside in their own worlds, and other beings may have doubts about this, or, again, they may not. Therefore, without giving way to our surprise and doubt, we should study the words, "mountains flow," with the Buddhas and Ancestors. Taking one (view), there is flowing; taking another, there is nonflowing. At one time there is flowing; at another, not-flowing. If our study is not like this, it is not the true dharma wheel of the Tathagatha.

An ancient Buddha has said, "If you wish to avoid the karma of hell, do not slander the true dharma wheel of the Tathagatha." These words should be engraved on skin, flesh, bones, and marrow, engraved on interior and exterior of body and mind, engraved on emptiness and on form; they are engraved on tree and rocks, engraved on fields and villages.

Although we say that mountains belong to the country, actually they belong to those who love them. When the mountains love their master, the wise and the virtuous inevitably enter the mountains. And when sages and wise ones live in the mountains, because the mountains belong to them, trees and rocks flourish and abound, and the birds and beasts take on a supernatural excellence. This is because the sages and wise ones have covered them with virtue. We should realize that the mountains actually take delight in wise ones and sages.

We should understand that the mountains are not within the human realm, nor within the realm of heaven. They are not to be viewed with the suppositions of human thought. If only we did not compare them with flowing in the human realm, who would have any doubt about such things as the mountains flowing or not flowing?

Again, since ancient times, wise ones and sages have also lived by the water. When they live by the water they catch fish, or they catch people, or they catch the Way. These are all traditional water styles. And going further, there must be catching the self, catching the hook, being caught by the hook, and being caught by the Way.

In ancient times when Te-ch'eng suddenly left Yueh-shan and went to live on the river, he got the sage of the Hua-t'ing River. Is this not catching fish? Is it not catching men? Catching water? Is it not catching himself? For someone to meet Te-ch'eng he must be Te-ch'eng; Te-ch'eng's teaching someone is his meeting himself.

It is not the case simply that there is water in the world; within the world of water there is a world. And this is true not only within water: within clouds as well there is a world of sentient beings; within wind, within fire, within earth there is a world of sentient beings. Within the dharma realm there is a world of sentient beings; within a single blade of grass, within a single staff there is a world of sentient beings. And wherever there is a world of sentient beings, there, inevitably, is the world of the Buddhas and Ancestors. This truth we should study very carefully.

Thus, water is the palace of the true dragon; it is not flowing away. If we regard it as only flowing, the word *flowing* is an insult to water; for it is (the same as) imposing *nonflowing*. Water is nothing but the real form of water just as it is. Water is the water virtue; it is not the flowing. In the thorough study of the flowing, or the nonflowing, of a single (drop of) water, the entirety of the ten thousand dharmas is instantly realized.

As for mountains, there are mountains hidden in jewels; there are mountains hidden in marshes, mountains hidden in the sky; there are mountains hidden in mountains. There is a study of mountains hidden in hiddenness. An ancient Buddha has said, "Mountains are mountains and rivers are rivers." The meaning of these words is not that mountains are mountains, but that mountains are mountains. Therefore, we should thoroughly study these mountains. When we thoroughly study the mountains, this is the mountain training. Such mountains and rivers themselves spontaneously become wise ones and sages.

ZAZEN CHECKLIST

The following checklist will help you to learn to arrange yourself in a good posture for sitting zazen. Assuming a comfortable, stable body position that you can maintain for the duration of a sitting period will form a sound basis for your practice.

1. Sit on the forward third of your zafu, using the cushion as a wedge. This will help relieve some strain on your back and allow you to sit with your torso centered. It will also put some pressure in your *hara*, the lower abdomen.

2. Except when sitting in a chair, arrange your legs to make your body into a pyramid, with both knees and buttocks in contact with the floor. Full lotus, half lotus, Burmese, and seiza (kneeling) positions are all equally acceptable. When sitting in a chair, use your back rather than the chair's back to support yourself. Sit far enough forward so you can place both of your feet flat on the floor.

3. Center your spine by swaying in decreasing arcs.

4. Straighten and align your spine by extending it and pushing the top of your head toward the ceiling while tucking your chin in a little, then relaxing your weight. The origin of the thrust is at the small of the back, with buttocks protruding slightly back and the lower belly forward. Your back should be erect but not rigid or tense.

5. Your head should rest squarely on your spine and should not tilt forward, backward, or to either side. Ears should be parallel with the shoulders. Tip of the nose is centered over the navel. Your spine, not your neck muscles, should be doing all of the work of supporting your head.

6. Sit with your eyes neither fully opened nor fully closed, but lowered at a 45-degree angle, and unfocused, "gazing" at the floor three to four feet in front of you. If you are sitting right next to the wall, look "through" it to where the floor would be.

7. Lips are kept closed, with your teeth pressed lightly together. Place your tongue against the roof of the mouth, just behind the front teeth. Swallow any saliva and breathe out once through your mouth, creating a slight vacuum which will inhibit salivation. Begin breathing through your nose.

8. Hands are placed in the "cosmic" mudra — right hand palm up with its blade against your lower belly, left hand, also palm up, resting on the right hand, middle knuckles overlapping and the thumbs lightly touching at the tips. If you are left handed, then let the right hand rest on top of the left. The mudra should look like an oval nestled against your lower abdomen.

9. Keep absolutely still throughout the period of zazen.

INTRODUCTION TO THE ZENDO (MEDITATION HALL)

1. **Dress and Deportment**: Dress neatly and move with attentiveness. Zazen robes are required for those who have them; clean, loose-fitting, quietly-colored clothing for those who do not. Remove your shoes before entering the hall and store them in the shoe racks. Do not wear jewelry, hats, tank tops, T-shirts with messages, perfume, or cologne. Make sure that wrist watches with alarms are turned off. Your dress should in no way call attention to itself or disturb the spirit of harmony in the zendo.

2. **Entering and Leaving**: Be very conscious of your decision to do this practice. When entering the zendo, put your palms together, elbows spread apart so your forearms are almost parallel to the ground, and bow. This is "gassho," an expression and practice of identification and unity. When you have found your seat — the rectangular black mat (*zabuton*) and the round black cushion (*zafu*) — gassho to it, then turn and gassho to the sitters across from you in the zendo. If you are using a bench or a chair, now is the time to get one from the back of the zendo. Once seated, return the bow of those who arrive at seats in front of and beside you. When the final meditation period has ended and it is time to leave, straighten your pillows, bow to them, return your bench or chair if you used one, and as you reach the entryway, face the altar and bow prior to leaving the room.

3. **Posture for Zazen**: Good posture and breathing are very important to the process of zazen. Posture should

express the vigor and the attentiveness of your practice —
sit straight; don't slump or allow yourself to sway with
drowsiness. Breathing should be slow, smooth, quiet,
and deep. Relax your muscles and concentrate your
mind, putting yourself entirely into your practice. It is
essential to remain perfectly still for the period of meditation. When the body moves, the mind moves. The point
of zazen is to experience the stillness of the mind.

4. **Zazen**: Each period of zazen begins with three strikes
on a bell and generally lasts thirty-five minutes, ending
with two bell sounds. Once the period has begun, do not
move until the bell is struck by the time-keeper to end the
period. During these periods stay with your practice, do
zazen; don't look around, worry about the time, adjust
your posture, think. This is time you have committed to
zazen. Please, do not waste it.

5. *Kinhin* **(Walking Meditation)**: This is the first opportunity to take the concentration and attention of zazen
into movement. Kinhin is not a "break" but a vital part of
the training in the zendo. When the meditation period
ends, gassho, then get up slowly so that the circulation in
your legs normalizes. Bow to your seat and turn to face
the center of the zendo. Stand in front of your seat, hands
held in gassho. Be mindful of all your movements. When
the wooden clappers are hit, bow, and those in the front
rows on either side of the zendo turn to their right, those
in the back rows turn to their left. When the clappers are
hit again, put your hands at your waist in "shasshu" —
left hand in a fist with thumb tucked in, right hand
encircling the left. Begin walking very slowly, half a step
forward with each cycle of breathing. Eyes are kept
lowered and concentration is maintained. When the clappers are hit again, bow from the waist, then begin to walk

at a brisk pace, staying right behind the person walking in front of you. As you pass by zendo exits during this fast-walking period, you may leave to use the bathrooms. Return promptly to your place in line; kinhin lasts approximately five minutes. When the clappers sound again, place your hands back in gassho and continue walking until you reach your seat. Gassho to your seat and turn to face the center of the zendo. At the sound of the bell, bow, and resume sitting.

6. *Kyosaku*: The *kyosaku* (long flat stick carried by zendo monitors during periods of zazen) is used only when a sitter explicitly requests it for relief of shoulder, back, or neck tension. Its use is an expression of compassion. To request the kyosaku, put your hands in gassho as the monitor approaches your seat. When the monitor stops either in front or behind you, the two of you bow *together*. Offer one shoulder by bending your head to the side and then offer the other. After the monitor has struck both shoulder acupressure points, bow again and the monitor will move on. The snap of the kyosaku serves to keep the atmosphere in the zendo crisp and awake.

7. *Dokusan/Daisan* (**Face-to-Face Teaching**): During some periods of zazen, Zen Mountain Monastery students will be called for private interview with the teacher. During certain retreats the opportunity for *dokusan* will be extended to non-students. The teacher's attendant (*jisha*) will let you know if this is open to you, and go over the formal procedures of the interview at that time.

8. **Buddhist Services**: Zen liturgy is a part of the training at Zen Mountain Monastery. You are asked to join with us in the chanting and the bowing, following the example of the monks and the senior students in the

zendo. Chanting should be done wholeheartedly but without shouting. The full bow, done most often in a sequence of three bows facing the altar, is an expression of unity between oneself and the Buddha, "the awakened one." To do the full bow, start with a standing bow, lowering yourself gently down to your knees. Touch your forehead and elbows to the ground and raise your hands, palms up and parallel to the floor, to ear level — a gesture of "raising the Buddha mind." Get up carefully and finish with a standing bow. The attitude of mind during the services is one of identification and gratitude.

JUKAI: TAKING THE PRECEPTS

INVOCATION OF THE THREE TREASURES

Be one with the Buddha in the ten directions
Be one with the Dharma in the ten directions
Be one with the Sangha in the ten directions
Be one with our original teacher Shakyamuni Buddha
Be one with Great Compassionate
Avalokiteshvara Bodhisattva
Be one with Great Wise Samantabhadra Bodhisattva
Be one with Great Holy Manjushri Bodhisattva
Be one with Koso Joyo Daishi (Dogen Zenji)
Be one with Taiso Josai Daishi (Keizan Zenji)
Be one with the Successive Great Ancestors

GATHA OF ATONEMENT

All evil karma committed by me since of old
Because of my beginningless greed, anger, and ignorance
Born of my body, mouth, and thought
Now I atone for it all

THE THREE TREASURES

I take refuge in the Buddha
I take refuge in the Dharma
I take refuge in the Sangha

I take refuge in the Buddha
The incomparably honored one
I take refuge in the Dharma, honorable for its purity
I take refuge in the Sangha, honorable for its harmony

I have taken refuge in the Buddha
I have taken refuge in the Dharma
I have taken refuge in the Sangha

THE THREE PURE PRECEPTS

1. Not Creating Evil
2. Practicing Good
3. Actualizing Good For Others

THE TEN GRAVE PRECEPTS

1. Affirm life; Do not kill
2. Be giving; Do not steal
3. Honor the body; Do not misuse sexuality
4. Manifest truth; Do not lie
5. Proceed clearly; Do not cloud the mind
6. See the perfection; Do not speak of others
   errors and faults
7. Realize self and other as one; Do not elevate the
   self and blame others
8. Give generously; Do not be withholding
9. Actualize harmony; Do not be angry
10. Experience the intimacy of things; Do not
    defile the Three Treasures

GATHA ON RECEIVING THE PRECEPTS

When sentient beings receive the Sila (Precepts)
They enter the realm of the Buddhas
Which is none other than The Great Enlightenment
Truly, they are the children of the Buddha

THE FOUR GREAT VOWS

Sentient beings are numberless; I vow to save them
Desires are inexhaustible; I vow to put an end to them
The Dharmas are boundless; I vow to master them
The Buddha Way is unattainable; I vow to attain it

DAILY LITURGY

MAHA PRAJNA PARAMITA HEART SUTRA

Avalokiteshvara Bodhisattva, doing deep Prajna Paramita
Clearly saw emptiness of all the five conditions
Thus completely relieving misfortune and pain
Oh Shariputra, form is no other than emptiness
Emptiness no other than form
Form is exactly emptiness, emptiness exactly form
Sensation, conception, discrimination, awareness
Are likewise like this
Oh Shariputra, all dharmas are forms of emptiness
Not born, not destroyed, not stained, not pure
Without loss, without gain
So in emptiness there is no form
No sensation, conception, discrimination, awareness
No eye, ear, nose, tongue, body, mind
No color, sound, smell, taste, touch, phenomena
No realm of sight, no realm of consciousness
No ignorance and no end to ignorance
No old age and death and no end to old age and death
No suffering, no cause of suffering
No extinguishing, no path
No wisdom and no gain
No gain and thus the Bodhisattva lives Prajna Paramita
With no hindrance in the mind
No hindrance therefore no fear
Far beyond deluded thoughts, this is Nirvana
All past, present, and future Buddhas live Prajna Paramita

And therefore attain anuttara-samyaksambodhi
Therefore know Prajna Paramita is the great mantra
The vivid mantra, the best mantra
The unsurpassable mantra
It completely clears all pain; this is the truth not a lie
So set forth the Prajna Paramita mantra
Set forth this mantra and say
Gate! Gate! Paragate!
Parasamgate! Bodhi Svaha!
Prajna Heart Sutra.

IDENTITY OF RELATIVE AND ABSOLUTE

The mind of the great sage of India
Was intimately conveyed from West to East.
Among human beings are wise ones and fools,
But in the Way there is no northern
Or southern patriarch.
The subtle source is clear and bright,
The tributary streams flow through the darkness.
To be attached to things is illusion,
To encounter the absolute is not yet enlightenment.
Each and all, the subjective and objective
Spheres are related,
And at the same time independent.
Related and yet working differently,
Though each keeps its own place.
Form makes the character and appearance different;
Sounds distinguish comfort and discomfort.
The dark makes all words one,
The brightness distinguishes good and bad phrases.
The four elements return to their nature
As a child to its mother.
Fire is hot, wind moves, water is wet, earth hard.
Eyes see, ears hear, nose smells,

Tongue tastes the salt and sour.
Each is independent of the other.
Cause and effect must return to the great reality.
The words high and low are used relatively.
Within light there is darkness,
But do not try to understand that darkness.
Within darkness there is light,
But do not look for that light.
Light and darkness are a pair,
Like the foot before and the foot behind in walking.
Each thing has its own intrinsic value
And is related to everything else in function and position.
Ordinary life fits the absolute as a box and its lid.
The absolute works together with the relative
Like two arrows meeting in midair.
Reading words you should grasp the great reality.
Do not judge by any standards.
If you do not see the Way,
You do not see it even as you walk on it.
When you walk the Way, it is not near, it is not far.
If you are deluded,
You are mountains and rivers away from it.
I respectfully say to those who wish to be enlightened,
Do not waste your time by night or day.

EMMEI JUKKU KANNON GYO

Kan ze on na mu butsu yo butsu u in yo butsu u en bup
po so en jo raku ga jo cho nen kan ze on bo nen kan ze on
nen nen ju shin ki nen nen fu ri shin.

Kan ze on na mu butsu yo butsu u in yo butsu u en bup
po so en jo raku ga jo cho nen kan ze on bo nen kan ze on
nen nen ju shin ki nen nen fu ri shin.

Kan ze on na mu butsu yo butsu u in yo butsu u en bup po so en jo raku ga jo cho nen kan ze on bo nen kan ze on nen nen ju shin ki nen nen fu ri shin.

SHO SAI MYO KICHIJO DHARANI

No mo san man da moto nan oha ra chi koto sha sono nan to ji to en gya gya gya ki gya ki un nun shiu ra shiu ra hara shiu ra hara shiu ra chishu sa chishu sa chishu ri chishu ri sowa ja sowa ja sen chi gya shiri ei somo ko.

No mo san man da moto nan oha ra chi koto sha sono nan to ji to en gya gya gya ki gya ki un nun shiu ra shiu ra hara shiu ra hara shiu ra chishu sa chishu sa chishu ri chishu ri sowa ja sowa ja sen chi gya shiri ei somo ko.

No mo san man da moto nan oha ra chi koto sha sono nan to ji to en gya gya gya ki gya ki un nun shiu ra shiu ra hara shiu ra hara shiu ra chishu sa chishu sa chishu ri chishu ri sowa ja sowa ja sen chi gya shiri ei somo ko.

VERSE OF THE KESA
(chant three times)

Vast is the robe of liberation,
A formless field of benefaction.
I wear the Tathagatha's teachings,
Saving all sentient beings.

THE FOUR GREAT VOWS
(chant three times)

Sentient beings are numberless; I vow to save them.
Desires are inexhaustible; I vow to put an end to them.
The Dharmas are boundless; I vow to master them.
The Buddha Way is unattainable; I vow to attain it.

GATHA ON OPENING THE SUTRA

The Dharma, incomparably profound and infinitely subtle,
Is rarely encountered, even in millions of ages.
Now we see it, hear it, receive and maintain it.
May we completely realize the Tathagatha's true meaning.

MEAL GATHA

First, seventy-two labors brought us this food,
We should know how it comes to us.
Second, as we receive this offering,
We should consider
Whether our virtue and practice deserve it.
Third, as we desire the natural order of mind,
To be free from clinging,
We must be free from greed.
Fourth, to support our life, we take this food.
Fifth, to attain our way we take this food.
First, this food is for the Three Treasures.
Second, it is for our teachers, parents, nation,
And all sentient beings.
Third, it is for all beings in the three worlds.
Thus, we eat this food with everyone,
We eat to stop all evil, to practice good,
To save all sentient beings,
And to accomplish our Buddha Way.

DEDICATION

All Buddhas throughout space and time,
All Bodhisattva Mahasattvas,
Maha Prajna Paramita.

READING LIST

STAGE I

SUTRAS
The Diamond Sutra and The Sutra of Hui-neng, translated
   by A. F. Price and Wong Mou-lam, Shambhala

RECORDS OF MODERN MASTERS
On Zen Practice Series — Volumes 1–3, edited by Hakuyu
   Taizan Maezumi and Bernard Tetsugen Glassman,
   Center Publications/Zen Center of Los Angeles
The Hazy Moon of Enlightenment, Hakuyu Taizan
   Maezumi and Bernard Tetsugen Glassman,
   Center Publications
Taking the Path of Zen, Robert Aitken, North Point Press
Zen Mind, Beginner's Mind, Shunryu Suzuki, Weatherhill
The Three Pillars of Zen, edited by Philip Kapleau,
   Doubleday
Getting the Buddha Mind, Master Sheng-yen,
   Dharma Drum Publications

HISTORY
Zen and Japanese Culture, Daisetz T. Suzuki,
   Bollingen Series LXIV, Princeton University Press
How the Swans Came to the Lake, Rick Fields, Shambhala

PHILOSOPHY AND THEOLOGY
What the Buddha Taught, Walpola Rahula,
   Grove Weidenfeld Publishers

STAGE II

RECORDS OF THE ANCIENT MASTERS
The Platform Sutra of the Sixth Patriarch, translated by
Philip B. Yampolsky, Columbia University Press

SUTRAS
The Holy Teaching of Vimalakirti, translated by Robert A.
F. Thurman, The Pennsylvania State University Press

RECORDS OF MODERN MASTERS
Approach to Zen, Kosho Uchiyama Roshi,
Japan Publications
The Mind of Clover, Robert Aitken, North Point Press
Cutting Through Spiritual Materialism, Chögyam
Trungpa, Shambhala
The Myth of Freedom and the Way of Meditation,
Chögyam Trungpa, Shambhala
The Way of Everyday Life, Hakuyu Taizan Maezumi and
John Daido Loori, Center Publications
Mountain Record of Zen Talks, John Daido Loori,
Dharma Communications
Returning to Silence, Dainin Katagiri, Shambhala

HISTORY
A Survey of Buddhism, Sangharakshita,
Tharpa Publications

STAGE III

RECORDS OF THE ANCIENT MASTERS

*Swampland Flowers: The Letters and Lectures of Zen
    Master Ta Hui*, translated by Christopher Cleary,
    Grove Press
The Original Face: An Anthology of Rinzai Zen,
    translated by Thomas Cleary, Grove Press
Moon in a Dewdrop: Writings of Zen Master Dogen,
    edited by Kazuaki Tanahashi, North Point Press
*Cultivating the Empty Field: The Silent Illumination of
    Zen Master Hongzhi*, translated by Taigen Daniel
    Leighton with Yi Wu, North Point Press
*How to Raise an Ox: Zen Practice as Taught in
    Zen Master Dogen's Shobogenzo*, Francis Dojun Cook,
    Center Publications

SUTRAS

The Perfection of Wisdom in Eight Thousand Lines,
    Edward Conze, Four Seasons Foundation, California

ZMM KOAN COLLECTIONS

Twenty Koans after Kensho, Diamond Sangha
    translation, unpublished
One Hundred Miscellaneous Koans, Takuju Lineage,
    internal translation, unpublished

RECORDS OF MODERN MASTERS

The Zen Koan, Isshu Miura and Ruth Fuller Sasaki,
    Harcourt Brace Jovanovich
A Flower Does Not Talk, Abbot Zenkei Shibayama,
    Charles E. Tuttle Company
The Iron Flute, translated by Nyogen Senzaki and Ruth
    Strout McCandless, Charles E. Tuttle Company

HISTORY

Timeless Spring, translated by Thomas Cleary, Weatherhill

<u>STAGE IV</u>

RECORDS OF THE ANCIENT MASTERS
The Record of Tung-shan, translated by William F.
    Powell, University of Hawaii Press
The Record of Lin-Chi, Ruth Fuller Sasaki, The Institute
    for Zen Studies, Kyoto, Japan
The Zen Master Hakuin, translated by Philip B.
    Yampolsky, Columbia University Press
A Man of Zen: The Recorded Sayings of Layman P'ang,
    translated by Ruth Fuller Sasaki, Yoshitaka Iriya, and
    Dana R. Fraser, Weatherhill

SUTRAS
The Threefold Lotus Sutra, translated by Bunno Kato,
    Yoshiro Tamura and Kojiro Miyasaka, Weatherhill/Kosei

ZMM KOAN COLLECTIONS
Zen Comments on the Mumonkan, Zenkei Shibayama,
    Harper & Row

RECORDS OF MODERN MASTERS
*Like a Dream, Like a Fantasy: The Zen Writings and
    Translations of Nyogen Senzaki*, edited by Eido
    Shimano, Japan Publications
Golden Wind: Zen Talks by Eido Shimano Roshi,
    Eido Shimano, Japan Publications
Only Don't Know, Seung Sahn, Four Seasons Publishing

PHILOSOPHY AND THEOLOGY
Essays in Zen Buddhism by D.T. Suzuki, Grove Press
Essays in Zen Buddhism, 2nd series, D.T. Suzuki,
    Samuel Weiser, Inc.
Essays in Zen Buddhism, 3rd series, D.T. Suzuki,
    Rider and Company

STAGE V

RECORDS OF THE ANCIENT MASTERS
The Zen Teachings of Huang Po (Obaku), John Blofield,
    Grove Press
Bankei Zen (Record of Bankei), translated by Peter
    Haskel, Grove Press
The Unborn: The Life and Teaching of Zen Master Bankei,
    translated by Norman Waddell, North Point Press
Sounds of Valley Streams: Enlightenment in Dogen's Zen,
    Francis H. Cook, State University of New York Press

SUTRAS
The Lankavatara Sutra, translated by D.T. Suzuki,
    Routledge and Kagon Paul Limited, London

ZMM KOAN COLLECTIONS
The Blue Cliff Record, translated by Thomas Cleary and
    J. C. Cleary, Shambhala

RECORDS OF MODERN MASTERS
Zen is Eternal Life, Kennett Roshi, Dharma Publishing

HISTORY
Zen Buddhism: A History — Volumes 1 & 2,
    Heinrich Dumoulin, Macmillan Publishing Company
Buddhism, It's History and Development, Edward Conze,
    Harper & Row

STAGE VI

RECORDS OF THE ANCIENT MASTERS
The Sayings and Doings of Pai-Chang, Thomas Cleary,
    Center Publications
The Zen Teachings of Huai-Hai (Daibai), John Blofield,
    Writer & Co., London
Zen Dawn: Early Zen Texts from Tun Huang, translated
    by J. C. Cleary, Shambhala

SUTRAS
*The Flower Ornament Scripture: The Avatamsaka Sutra —
    Volumes 1–4*, translated by Thomas Cleary,
    Shambhala
Buddhist Abhidharma, U Kyaw Min, Heian Press

ZMM KOAN COLLECTIONS
Book of Equanimity: 100 Koans and Verses, internal
    translation, unpublished

RECORDS OF THE ANCIENT MASTERS
Original Teachings of Ch'an Buddhism: The Transmission of the Lamp, translated by Chang Chung-Yuan, Vintage Books, Random House

SUTRAS
The Flower Ornament Scripture: The Avatamsaka Sutra — Volumes 1–4, translated by Thomas Cleary, Shambhala

ZMM KOAN COLLECTIONS
Transmission of the Light: 52 Koans, internal translation, unpublished
The Record of Transmitting the Light: Zen Master Keizan's 'Denkoroku', translated by Francis H. Cook, Center Publications
Tung-shan's Five Ranks (Goi Koans), internal translation, unpublished

HISTORY
The Way of Korean Zen, Koo San, Weatherhill Press

PHILOSOPHY AND THEOLOGY
Zen and Western Thought, Masao Abe, University of Hawaii Press
Merton: A Biography, Furlong, Bantam Books
The Ascent to Truth, Thomas Merton, Harcourt Brace Jovanovich
Practical Mysticism, Evelyn Underhill, Dutton Paperback
The Spiritual Life, Evelyn Underhill, Harper & Row
Three Jewish Philosophers, Lewy, Meridian/Penguin Books

STAGE VIII

RECORDS OF THE ANCIENT MASTERS
The Sayings of Master Joshu, Yoel Hoffman,
  Autumn Press, Massachusetts
Every End Exposed (Kidogoroku), Yoel Hoffman,
  Autumn Press

SUTRAS
*The Flower Ornament Scripture: The Avatamsaka Sutra —
  Volumes 1–4*, translated by Thomas Cleary,
  Shambhala

ZMM KOAN COLLECTIONS
Koans of the Way of Reality, in-house publication

PHILOSOPHY AND THEOLOGY
*The Northern School and the Formation of Early Ch'an
  Buddhism*, McCrey, University of Hawaii Press
Buddhist Hermeneutics, Lopez, Kuroda Institute,
  University of Hawaii Press
Traditions in Meditation in Chinese Buddhism, Peter
  Kakuzen Gregory, Kuroda Institute, University of
  Hawaii Press
Dogen Studies, edited by William R. LaFleur, Kuroda
  Institute, University of Hawaii Press
Dogen Kigen: Mystical Realist, Hee-Jin Kim,
  The University of Arizona Press
Mysticism, Evelyn Underhill, Meridian/Penguin Books
The Social Organization of Zen Practice, Preston,
  Cambridge University Press

STAGE IX

RECORDS OF THE ANCIENT MASTERS
Dogen Zenji's Shobogenzo — Volumes 1–4, translated by
    Kosen Nishiyama, published by Nakayama Shobo
Eiheiji Goroku, translated by Yuho Yokoi, Sankibo Press
Eihei-Genzenji-Shingi by Eihei Dogen, translated
    by Yuho Yokoi, Sankibo Press

SUTRAS
*The Flower Ornament Scripture: The Avatamsaka Sutra —
    Volumes 1–4*, translated by Thomas Cleary,
    Shambhala

ZMM KOAN COLLECTIONS
Precept Koans, internal translation, unpublished

HISTORY
History of Zen, Y. H. Ku, published by the author,
    University of Pennsylvania

PHILOSOPHY AND THEOLOGY
Studies in Ch'an and Hua-yen, edited by Robert Gimello
    and Peter Kakuzen Gregory, Kuroda Institute,
    University of Hawaii Press
Hua-yen Buddhism, Francis Dojun Cook,
    The Pennsylvania State University Press
Shingon: Japanese Esoteric Buddhism, Taiko Yamasaki,
    Shambhala
Mandala Symbolism, C.G. Jung, Princeton University Press
The Theory and Practice of Mandala, Tucci,
    Samuel Weiser, Inc.
The Principles of Buddhist Psychology, Kalupahana,
    State University of New York Press

GLOSSARY

ABSOLUTE/RELATIVE: Perfectly interrelated, mutually arising aspects of reality; absolute is oneness, emptiness, the true nature of reality, while the relative is its phenomenal manifestation.

ANATMAN: No-self; the anatman doctrine is one of the essential teachings of Buddhism, stating that there is no permanent, enduring substance within any entity; self is an idea.

ANUTTARA-SAMYAKSAMBODHI: Supreme perfect enlightenment of a complete Buddha.

***BLUE CLIFF RECORD*:** A collection of one hundred koans compiled, with appreciatory verses, by Master Hsueh-tou Ch'ung-hsien, 980-1052 (Jap. Setcho Juken) and with commentaries by Master Yuan-wu K'o-Ch'in, 1063-1135 (Jap. Engo Kokugon); a key text in the Rinzai Zen School, it was studied byMaster Dogen, who carried a handwritten copy back to Japan from China.

BODHI MIND: Mind in which the aspiration for enlightenment has been awakened; the impulse that moves one towards self-realization.

BODHISATTVA: One who practices the Buddha Way and compassionately postpones final enlightenment for the sake of others; the ideal of practice in Mahayana Buddhism.

Bodhi Tree: The fig tree under which the historical Buddha, Siddhartha Gautama, attained complete enlightenment.

Buji Zen: Free-styled, non-conformist attitude toward Zen training that arises out of an intellectual misunderstanding of Zen practice and enlightenment.

Dana: Voluntary giving; considered in Buddhism as one of the most important virtues; one of the six paramitas, or perfections.

Dharani: A short sutra consisting of fundamental sounds that carry no extrinsic meaning.

Dharma: Universal truth or law; the Buddha's teachings; all phenomena that make up reality.

Dharma Combat: Unrehearsed dialogue in which two Zen practitioners test and sharpen their understanding of Zen truths.

Dharma Discourse: A formal talk on a koan or significant aspects of Zen teachings; not an intellectual presentation or a philosophical explanation, but a direct expression of the spirit of Zen by the teacher.

Dharmakaya: One of the three *kayas*, bodies of the Buddha; the body of the great order, essential reality; the unity of the Buddha with the existing universe.

Dharma Name: Name given to a student by the teacher during *jukai*, the precepts ceremony.

Dogen Kigen Zenji: (1200-1253) Founder of the Japanese Soto School of Zen; Dogen established Eihei-ji, the principal Soto training monastery in Japan; he is the author of the *Shobogenzo*, an important collection of Dharma essays.

Dokusan/Daisan: Private interviews with the teacher during which students present and clarify their understanding of the Dharma.

Dragons and Snakes: Enlightened and deluded beings; in Zen writings dragons frequently represent true adepts while snakes denote people who hold and expound spurious views.

Eightfold Path: The content of the Buddha's Fourth Noble Truth, the way out of suffering; it consists of right views, right determination, right speech, right action, right livelihood, right effort, right mindfulness, and right concentration; some translators replace "right" with "perfect" to avoid dualistic connotations.

Eight Gates of Training: Training system used at Zen Mountain Monastery for complete living and realization; it includes zazen, Zen study with the teacher, academic study, liturgy, precepts practice, art practice, body practice, and work practice; it corresponds roughly to the aspects of the Buddha's Eightfold Path.

Enlightenment: The direct experience of one's true nature.

Five Ranks of Tung-shan: A system of understanding existence's two components, the interplay of the absolute and the relative, developed by the Chinese Zen Master

Tung-shan Liang-chieh in the ninth century; it is also a formulation of different degrees of enlightenment.

FOUR NOBLE TRUTHS: The first teaching of the historical Buddha; it addresses the nature of all suffering and points to the way of overcoming suffering; the Truths are: (1) life is suffering, (2) suffering has a cause, (3) there is an end to the cause of suffering, (4) the way to put an end to suffering is the Eightfold Path.

FOUR VOWS: Vows taken by the bodhisattvas, expressing commitment to postpone their own enlightenment until all beings are liberated from delusion; they are chanted at the end of each day at Zen monasteries.

FUSATSU: Renewal of vows; a ceremony and a service, conducted periodically at monasteries, during which practitioners atone for their deluded actions and resolve to continue on the path of self-realization.

GASSHO: Gesture of bringing one's hands together, palm to palm, embodying the identity of all dualities.

GATHA: Short sutra that presents the Dharma teachings in terse, pithy wording; frequently chanted.

GENJOKOAN: THE WAY OF EVERYDAY LIFE: The first fascicle and the heart of Dogen Zenji's master-work, *Shobogenzo*.

HARA: Physical and spiritual center of one's body/mind; area in the lower belly used in centering one's attention in meditation and any activity.

HOSSU: Fly-whisk; a short staff with animal hair attached to one end; it was originally used by monks in

India to shoo away insects; in Zen tradition it is passed on from a teacher to a student who is a Dharma successor, and has received mind-to-mind transmission.

Joriki: Power of concentration, developed through the practice of meditation, that allows a person to place their focus of attention where they choose for extended periods of time.

Jukai: Acknowledgment of and the reception of the Buddhist precepts; the ceremony of becoming a Buddhist.

Karma: The universal law of cause and effect, linking an action's underlying intention to that action's consequences; it equates the actions of body, speech, and thought as potential sources of karmic consequences.

Kensho: "Seeing into one's own nature"; first experience of realization.

Kesa: Monk's outer robe, worn across one shoulder.

Ki: Vital life-force present in and permeating all things; the energy which is the source of all creative activity.

Kinhin: Walking meditation; it provides a transitional stage for shifting the concentration developed in zazen into activity.

Koan: An apparently paradoxical statement or question used in Zen training to induce in the student an intense level of doubt, allowing them to cut through conventional and conditioned descriptions of reality and see directly into their true nature.

KOANS OF THE WAY OF REALITY: A collection of 108 Zen koans, together with prologue, capping verse, and footnotes, culled from ancient and modern sources that are particularly relevant to Zen practitioners today. It is part of koan study at Zen Mountain Monastery.

KYOSAKU: "Wake-up stick"; a flattened stick used by the monitors in the zendo to strike acupressure points on a person's shoulders, relieving tension and promoting wakefulness.

MAHAYANA: "Great vehicle"; the northern school of Buddhism that expresses and aims at the intrinsic connection between an individual's realization and the simultaneous enlightenment of all beings.

MONDO: An informal, free-wheeling dialogue between the teacher and the students that centers on some relevant aspect of the teachings.

MOUNTAINS AND RIVERS SUTRA: A chapter in the *Shobogenzo* depicting the interrelatedness of the absolute and the relative.

MU: One of the first koans used in koan training; the first case in Master Wu-men's *Gateless Gate* collection of koans.

NIRVANA: Union with the absolute; in Zen it is essential to realize that samsara is nirvana, form is emptiness, that all beings are innately perfect from the outset.

ORYOKI: "Containing just enough"; set of bowls and the ceremonial meal eaten in silence in Buddhist monasteries.

266 THE EIGHT GATES OF ZEN

Paramitas: Perfections; virtues of attitude and behavior cultivated by bodhisattvas in the course of their development, necessary on the path of transcendence or realization; "reaching the other shore"; the six paramitas are generosity, discipline, patience, exertion, meditation, and wisdom.

Prajna: Wisdom; not that which is possessed but that which is directly and thoroughly experienced.

Precepts: Moral and ethical guidelines that, in Buddhism, are a description of the life of a Buddha, one who realizes the nature of existence and acts out of that realization.

Rakusu: The miniaturized version of the kesa, a bib-shaped garment worn by Zen Buddhist practitioners across their chest.

Rinzai School: School of Zen that originated with the great Chinese Zen Master Lin-chi I-hsuan in the ninth century and was reformed by Master Hakuin in Japan; it stresses koan practice.

Roshi: "Old venerable master"; title of Zen teachers.

Samadhi: State in which the mind is absorbed in intense concentration, free from distractions and goals; the essential nature of the self can be experienced directly within samadhi.

Samsara: Existence prior to liberation, conditioned by the three attitudes of greed, anger, and ignorance and marked by continuous rebirths.

Sangha: Community of practitioners; all sentient and insentient beings.

Satori: The experience of awakening; enlightenment.

Sesshin: "Gathering of the mind"; an extended period of intensive meditation practice lasting between five and ten days, centered on zazen but encompassing every aspect of the daily schedule.

Shakyamuni Buddha: Siddhartha Gautama, the historical Buddha and the founder of Buddhism; he was a prince of the Shakya clan, living in the northern India in the sixth century B.C.

Shikantaza: "Just sitting"; form of zazen in which one practices pure awareness.

Shobogenzo: "Treasury of the True Dharma Eye"; a collection of writings and discourses of the Japanese Master Eihei Dogen.

Soto School: One of the existing schools of Zen Buddhism, founded by the Chinese Masters Tung-shan Liang-chieh and Ts'ao-shan Pen-chi in ninth century; it was revitalized and brought to Japan by Eihei Dogen.

Sunyata: Void. Central principle of Buddhism that recognizes the emptiness of all composite entities, without reifying nothingness. Resolution of all dualities.

Sutra: Narrative text consisting chiefly of the discourses and teachings of the Buddha.

TAO: The Way, Truth, primary principle, universal reality, teaching; the nameless and the unnameable source of all things; key concept in Taoism and Zen.

TATHAGATHA: One of the titles of the Buddha, "thus-come one," referring to one who has attained the perfect enlightenment.

TEN DIRECTIONS: All-pervading space.

TEN OX-HERDING PICTURES: An ancient Chinese descriptive device; a collection of drawings with accompanying comments and poems that presents the progress of a person on the path of self-realization.

TEN STAGES: A schematic system delineating progressive phases of Zen training at Zen Mountain Monastery, based on the Ten Ox-Herding Pictures of Master K'uo-an.

TEN THOUSAND THINGS: The phenomenal universe of distinct entities.

TENZO: The chief cook of the monastery; usually a senior monk or roshi who uses the context of food preparation and serving as skillful means for teaching those working with him or her.

THREE PILLARS OF PRACTICE: The essential components of the Zen path of realization — great doubt, great faith, and great perseverance.

THREE POISONS: Greed, anger, and ignorance; characteristics of human existence that arise out of the deluded view of the universe.

Three Treasures: Buddha, Dharma, and Sangha; one who is awakened, the true teachings, and the group of people living in accord with the teachings; the Treasures are also known as the places of refuge for Buddhist practitioners.

Tokudo: Ceremony of ordination.

Transmission: Complete, mind-to-mind merging of the teacher and the student; the confirmation of a student's realization.

Upaya: Skillful means; forms that the teachings take, reflecting their appropriateness to the circumstances in which they appear.

Verse of the Kesa: Short sutra chanted after the morning meditation period, expressing one's identification with the teachings of the Buddha.

Vinaya: School of Buddhism that centers its practice on strict and precise observance of monastic rules and ethical precepts; collection of Buddhist precepts.

Zafu: Round pillow used in sitting meditation.

Zendo: Meditation hall.

ABOUT
ZEN MOUNTAIN MONASTERY

Zen Mountain Monastery is an American Zen Buddhist monastery and training center for monks and lay practitioners. It is located on a 230-acre site on Tremper Mountain in New York's Catskill Mountains, surrounded by state forest wilderness and featuring an Environmental Studies Area. The Monastery provides a year-round daily training program that includes Zen meditation, various forms of face-to-face teaching, academic studies, liturgy, work practice, body practice, art practice, and study of the Buddhist precepts. Each month an introductory weekend Zen training workshop, and a week-long silent Zen meditation retreat *(sesshin)* are offered. During the spring and fall quarters of each year, ninety-day intensive programs *(Ango)* are conducted. Throughout the year, the regular daily schedule is supplemented with seminars and workshops in the Zen arts, the martial arts, Buddhist studies, and other areas relevant to present-day, Western practitioners. Students can train in either full-time or part-time residency or as non-residents whose "home practice" is fueled by periodic visits to the Monastery.

For further information, contact:

REGISTRAR
ZEN MOUNTAIN MONASTERY
P.O. BOX 197
MOUNT TREMPER, NY 12457
(914) 688-2228